D1593766

THE
MODERN
LAW FIRM

THE MODERN LAW FIRM

HOW TO THRIVE IN AN ERA OF RAPID TECHNOLOGICAL CHANGE

HEINAN LANDA

optimal networks books

—2020—

The Modern Law Firm: How to Thrive in an Era of Rapid Technological Change
by Heinan Landa
Published by Optimal Networks Books
15201 Diamondback Drive, Suite 220
Rockville, Maryland 20850

ISBN: 978-1-7345764-0-5 hardcover
978-1-7345764-1-2 trade paperback
978-1-7345764-2-9 electronic book
First printing
MANUFACTURED IN THE THE UNITED STATES OF AMERICA
Design and composition: www.dmargulis.com
Cover and title page design: Metadog Design Group

Contents

Preface

What does a thriving law firm look like in five years?
In a word: different.

Over the three decades I've spent in Information Technology, I have never seen such rapid and dramatic changes in technology and its impact on our daily lives. And across the three decades I've spent serving law firms, I have never seen such unease surrounding the future of the legal industry. Here are some of the things I hear clients say:

- *We used to have maybe three or four real firms to compete with. Now there are twenty, thirty other firms in the area, and we're all going after the same business. How do we differentiate ourselves in a way that actually means something to our clients?*

- *There's this palpable tension between how our firm works and how our clients expect us to work. They want answers immediately, they want results immediately, and more often than not, that just isn't possible. How are we supposed to keep up?*

- *The pace of work has gone completely through the roof. We can already get so much more work done in a day than we used to, but it still feels like we're never quite going fast enough, never making enough progress. It's exhausting. Is this just how it's going to be from now on?*

- *We have these young associates walking into our firm, and they act like they've walked into the Twilight Zone or something. They look at our technology with this mix of confusion and exasperation on their faces. I know we don't have the latest and greatest, but are we really in such bad shape compared to other firms like ours?*

■ *With all these new firms popping up left and right, there's not just the risk of losing clients—there's the risk of losing our people, too. And our younger associates quite literally embody the future value of our firm. What can we do to keep the new talent we bring aboard?*

■ *Everything we do is under a microscope. Any misstep with a client and any conflict with an employee can wind up as a nasty review online— and all anyone can see is their side of the story. Are we really at the point where one disgruntled person can cost us business? Cost us new hires?*

Law firm leaders come to me frustrated, overwhelmed, and anxious. They have practices full of brilliant, hard-working people. They've accumulated years of successes and accolades. They are steadfastly devoted to the success of their firms and are doing everything in their power to ensure a bright and profitable future. But they can see trouble brewing. And it all comes down to technology.

I founded my outsourced technology firm, Optimal Networks, in 1991. Back then, providing technology support to law firms meant sending a network engineer to your offices once a month to check your servers, swap out your backup tapes, and give your secretary a hand with some glitch in WordPerfect. Technology played an important but small role in the firm's overall operations, meaning that my company played an important but small role in the firm's overall success.

Fast-forward to 2015: A law firm reached out to me for help. Thanks to a poorly architected cloud solution and equally poor support, they were losing $100,000 in billable time each and every month. Their clients were quickly losing patience with the firm's inability to provide responsive service. To top it off, the attorneys were so sick of fighting against their technology, having to devise their own workarounds, and falling behind on their work that firm morale had reached an all-time low. This firm was now looking to me to help them recover their revenue, mend their reputation, and prevent their people from walking out the door. Their business was in jeopardy as a direct result of their technology—and improving their technology would be their only saving grace.

That's why I'm writing this book. Technology now plays a central, dominant role in how we live and how we do business. It can singlehandedly bring an otherwise healthy law firm to the brink of failure. And on the flip side, it can empower firms to achieve a level of success that its leaders might not have thought possible. My goal is to provide your firm with the clarity and the tools to do the latter.

This book is organized in four parts:

1 **A Shifting Landscape**: We'll examine how law firms have traditionally operated, why this approach won't work going forward, and what your firm stands to lose if you stick with the status quo.

2 **From Threat to Asset**: We'll discuss how a shift in focus—powered by technology—will allow you to convert this new terrain from a series of stumbling blocks into a competitive advantage.

3 **Building the Foundation**: Next, we'll assess your firm's baseline Technology Operational Maturity Level and determine which critical gaps might need to be addressed before we can realistically dig into more complex initiatives.

4 **Realizing the Vision**: Finally, I'll recommend specific solutions and strategies as they relate to our vision and discuss how to get your whole firm on board with the changes ahead of them.

Along the way, I'll be drawing on several main sources of data:

■ Thirty years of my own experience in meeting the technology needs of law firms in the Washington, D.C., Metro area

■ As many years running a nationally and globally ranked professional services firm

- My team's collective technical and strategic expertise (which totals over 200 years of combined tenure at Optimal alone—not to mention their previous work experience!)

- Formal interviews with a generational cross-section of partners, lawyers, and Firm Administrators, combined with a number of more informal discussions I've had with clients of mine, members of our local Bar Associations, and members of our local chapter of the Association of Legal Administrators

- Research, research, and more research

Because my involvement in the industry has been focused on small to medium-sized firms (say, ten to one hundred attorneys), that's the size and perspective I'll speak about. Solo practitioners and large firms may still find value throughout this book, but the content will resonate most with those in the middle.

So, while my background is technical, this will not be a technical read—you need not have any expertise in technology to make sense of the pages that follow. Instead, I'm putting on my "founder & CEO, Wharton MBA" cap and approaching this book from a business perspective. Technology is only as valuable as the business results it helps you realize—increased revenue, decreased risk, or improved morale, for example.

Naturally, not everything in this book will apply to every firm. You may have already implemented some of the solutions or strategies I will talk about. You may have found another way to creatively address the vulnerabilities I will uncover. If that is the case, excellent—you are ahead of the curve.

More than anything, I hope to alleviate any anxiety you might be feeling and to replace all of that uncertainty with the confidence that your firm will not only weather these changes, but also come out on the other side stronger and more profitable than ever.

PART 1

A Shifting Landscape

Your Law Firm, Two Decades Ago

T he late '90s and early 2000s weren't all that long ago, especially when you consider that the legal profession has its roots in third-century Greece and Rome. The last twenty years make up just over *1 percent* of the entire history of the industry, but boy, have things changed during that time.

When I conducted interviews for this book, I asked each person to think back twenty years (or, for the younger crowd, as far back as they possibly could) and tell me what that time was like. How did they get their work done? How did they interact with people inside and outside the firm? What was the atmosphere? Their experiences have helped shape the snapshots that follow, which in turn will shape our discussion of how quickly and how massively the landscape has evolved over such a short period of time.

See if any of these scenarios sound familiar.

Identifying a Potential New Client

"Bill's going to *what* tonight?" The associate raised an eyebrow.

"*Network*. You know, meet people. Schmooze. Find more clients."

An attorney chimed in playfully: "If you've gotta hunt for them, you're doing something wrong!"

You hadn't heard of very many lawyers networking. Certainly not partners—they wouldn't *dream* of doing such a thing. Almost 100 percent of the firm's clients had come in by referral. They had been given your name by a friend, a colleague, a family member, or whomever, and they were hoping that you could help them with X, Y, and Z because yeesh, were they in some hot water.

You commended Bill for experimenting, but would stick to having your clients come to you, not the other way around.

Winning That Client's Business

You couldn't remember the last time you had to run through your qualifications. It happened every now and again, but most of your potential clients already "knew" you through friends or colleagues. Plus, when they visited your office to make things official, they could see the framed certificates plain as day. You didn't get too many questions about your rates, either. When you did, clients seemed to have two conflicting reactions simultaneously: (1) *Yikes!* and (2) *If they cost that much, they must be good!*

Really, your clients just wanted to feel like you understood their problems and were confident you could fix them. They'd pay what it took and leave the details to the experts. Besides, their friends wouldn't have sent them to someone who couldn't get the job done.

Securing Repeat Business

You took out your stationery set and your favorite pen. You had just won a case and always liked to close out your engagements with a little extra flair. Your secretary always told you it wasn't really necessary, but what could it hurt? It only took a couple minutes all told.

Kim,

Congratulations on your win! I told you we could do it.

If you or someone you know needs help down the road, you know where to find me.

Sincerely...

Catching Up on Missed Communications

Monday morning, 9:00. You settled into your desk chair, fired up the desktop computer (it took a while to get going), and rifled through the stack of pink notes your secretary had left for you. She had transcribed the voicemail messages from your missed calls—one from Friday evening and a few from over the weekend. None were urgent, of course; it wouldn't be much use for anyone to make demands of your answering service. You'd give these folks a call back in an hour, maybe two.

After your computer finally booted up, you logged into your electronic mailbox to see if a note or two had trickled in since you had checked last Friday, though you didn't usually get many messages outside of business hours.

Having a Conversation with Another Attorney

"Is Jean around?" You popped your head out of your office to ask your secretary, who shrugged in reply.

"I saw her grabbing coffee earlier today, but she might've left since."

The search began.

You wanted to discuss a client matter with Jean, who had worked through a similar situation before. She hadn't picked up when you called her desk. But that was a few minutes ago, so maybe she'd be back by now?

You walked down the hall to her office. Empty. An associate passed by, and you asked him if he knew where you might find her.

"No, sorry. Maybe she's in the kitchen for a fresh cup?"

On your way to the opposite end of the floor, you heard Jean's voice coming from another attorney's office. You knocked at the doorway.

"Sorry to interrupt. Jean, will you have a minute for me this afternoon?"

She checked her watch. "I need about an hour. Will that work?"

You checked your watch. "That should be fine, yes. I'll meet you in your office."

Back to your desk for now, then. Well, since you were already here, you might as well make a quick pit stop in the kitchen.

Doing Research

You decided to check in on your new paralegal, who was still learning the ropes. That afternoon she'd be tasked with going to the "library" (your conference room, really—it was lined with shelves upon shelves of reference binders) to research: finding headnotes in the right categories, checking the indices for the right subject matter, identifying which cases would be worth reading through, going to the shelf and pulling all the books, and then Shepardizing the case to see what *other* cases cited that case and whether or not it had actually proven useful. The standard process.

You'd heard rumors that LexisNexis was releasing a new tool that would allow you to enter a string of words into the platform and have your computer pull a set of cases and legislation that used those same words. It would do all the work itself. For now, though, you needed help getting this research done—it would take hours that you didn't have to spare.

Finding a Document

The document wasn't in the file folder. You sighed, took a deep breath to calm yourself.

The same thing had happened last week, and you *really* hoped it wouldn't be the same ten-minute ordeal this time. You needed to get a document together, and you knew there was an old document that would get you halfway there; why re-create the wheel when you don't have to?

When you had gone to pull that document from the file cabinet last week, it hadn't been there. The attorney who had created it said he didn't have it. He thought his secretary might. She didn't. The three of you went searching. An associate pitched in. You kept searching.

Ten minutes later, where did the file end up being? On the attorney's desk all along.

Here's hoping you could *bill* that ten minutes this time around.

Collaborating on a Document

"Will you be at your office for the next half-hour? I want to fax over the latest version of the document."

You had already made it through a couple rounds of revisions, but needed to make sure your client was on board with a few more changes you'd made.

"I'll mark it up so you can see what's different," you told him. "Write down any comments you have and fax it back to me, okay?"

There was a chance he'd get it back to you before you left for your appointment, but more than likely, your secretary would grab the fax off the machine and place it on your desk, where it would sit until the next morning. You'd give it a look and call your client's office with any questions. Fortunately, this client was pretty easy to reach—you almost never played phone tag with them.

From there, another round of internal reviews. You were probably three or four days away from having the final document ready to go.

Sending and Filing a Finished Document

You handed your dictation to your secretary. It was 1:00, and you needed this letter to go out with the day's post, which usually came around 2:00.

"I'll get started right away," she said, already making a beeline back to her computer.

Over the next hour, she listened to the recording and typed the letter in WordPerfect. (She was *much* faster on the keyboard than you, thankfully.) She printed the first draft on plain paper and brought it into your office. You marked up the page with your edits and walked the paper back to her. She applied those changes to the document, loaded the printer with official firm letterhead, printed the revised letter, and brought it to your office. Luckily, you were there to give it a final review and add your signature immediately. She made a copy of the signed letter for your records and put the original into an envelope that she addressed. Last step: postage. The letter made it into the outbound mail tray at 1:53. Just in time.

Shifts in the Way
We Do Business

To you younger readers, those snapshots likely paint a bizarre and unfamiliar picture. You might even have felt yourself getting impatient with the pace of it all. To you more venerable readers, I hope those scenarios tap into a few fond memories of "the good old days."

Those scenes encapsulate a few themes that were commonplace for most practices at the turn of the millennium:

- Building the firm's client base almost exclusively through word of mouth

- Loads of support staff and loads of paper

- Very little pressure to maximize firm efficiency (and much pressure to maximize billable time)

- Clear lines between business hours and after-hours

- Long-term loyalty from clients, attorneys, and staff alike

Over the past twenty years, however, this paradigm has been upended by two societal developments: the evolution of the Buyer's Journey, and the erosion of our collective patience.

Shift #1: The Evolution of the Buyer's Journey

The internet has singlehandedly upended the Buyer's Journey as we used to know it. Gone are the days when businesses and individuals would select their preferred representation based solely on the recommendation of a friend or colleague. Now, potential clients have instant and unfettered access to all kinds of information about your firm.

Think about it: Your prospective client has a business or personal challenge they believe they need legal advice to solve. What does their current journey look like?

Just as soon as they formulate that thought about seeking legal advice, they're probably going to hit the internet and search for local law firms that can solve their particular problem. Or perhaps they'll ask a friend or colleague for a recommendation, and then they'll hit the internet to investigate your firm for themselves. Or maybe they'll even meet one of your attorneys at a networking event and become interested in chatting further, in which case they'll probably search the internet when they get home.

In any case, you can bet your bottom dollar that they're going to end up on all those online review sites, on your firm's website, and probably on social media as well. What sort of story will these online resources tell about your firm? That your clients are raving fans? Your partners and attorneys have received ringing endorsements? Your win rate is off the charts? You have a long history of your collections outweighing your fees ten, a hundred, a thousand times over? You're a trusted thought leader in your area of law? Working with you will be painless? You're unquestionably the most qualified firm to solve your clients' problems and achieve the best results? They would be foolish not to pick up the phone or fill out a contact form to get in touch with you?

Or is the image you're projecting a bleaker one? Perhaps the few reviews you've gotten are unremarkable, suggesting that you do mediocre work. Or perhaps you make audacious, chest-thumping claims on your website, but have numerous negative reviews, suggesting that your firm is delusional at best and unethical at worst. Or maybe your website is clunky and difficult to navigate, suggesting that you aren't keeping up with the times and will probably be a pill to work with.

Here are some telling statistics:[1]

- Eighty-three percent of people who are looking for an attorney check lawyer reviews as the *first step* in that process.

- Seventy percent are willing to go to an attorney in an inconvenient location if that attorney has better reviews.

- Quality of service and years of experience are the two most important factors for clients when reading these reviews.

Sites like Yelp, Avvo, and Lawyers.com compile ratings for lawyers across the country, and potential clients are far more likely than not to read them before contacting your firm. In other words, a huge portion of the buying decision takes place *before you ever sit down with a potential client.* As Seth Berenzweig, Founding and Managing Partner of Berenzweig Leonard, puts it, "People come to the table smarter, and are asking smarter questions. They can do quick research with online tools at their desk or from their cell phone that can give them quick answers. It won't get them to the finish line, but we have a much more engaged audience."[2]

Roy Niedermayer, Principal with Paley Rothman, has seen a significant jump in the demand for more sophisticated digital and personal outreach over the past decade. "Some firms have visibility, but lawyers are feeling the pressure to blog and network," Niedermayer says. "Saying 'I'm a lawyer' and having people come to me doesn't work so much anymore."[3]

Because that's the way it was—years back, business development took the form of partners sitting at their desks and waiting for the phones to ring. Today, targeted outreach strategies are not only commonplace, they're critical; it's the firm with the most polished online presence, the best reviews, and the best-crafted brand that stands to win the most inbound leads. Building and maintaining your reputation has become a complex undertaking—it's not just the word of your friend or colleague;

it's the culmination of dozens upon dozens of data points strewn across the World Wide Web. You create some of these data points. Your attorneys and staff contribute others. Your clients create more still. This shift leaves you with so many opportunities to communicate your value to potential customers, so many avenues to promote your brand. It also presents so many opportunities to drive potential clients away.

This is a trend we're seeing across all industries. Between website overhauls, content marketing initiatives, and digital marketing campaigns (and, oh yeah, writing books), the amount of time and money I've invested in promoting Optimal online has increased dramatically over the past ten years. It's an investment I had to make if I had any intention of keeping pace with my competitors and with my potential clients' purchasing habits, never mind my ongoing desire to grow the company.

We as businesses have reached the point where a mediocre online presence will directly and instantly cost us clients. If an interested buyer visits our site to learn more about us and the homepage is sloppy and hard to navigate, they won't give it a second glance. If they can't get it to load properly on their smartphone or tablet, they're gone. If they don't walk away from your site with the confidence that you can solve their problems (i.e., that you'll be worth their investment), they aren't going to call you. It's that simple, and it's that extreme.

Shift #2: The Erosion of Our Collective Patience

So over the past twenty years, we as individuals have become a more connected and informed bunch, thanks to the World Wide Web. If we take a step back and look at the technology landscape as a whole over that same timespan, the advancements are nothing short of mind-blowing. Here are some of the biggest developments from the early 2000s to give you a sense of how far we've come:

- 2000: Congress approves GPS technology for public use, and text messaging goes mainstream.

- 2001: The iPod is released.

- 2002: Cell phones get cameras.

- 2004: The Google search engine launches for public use.

- 2005: YouTube launches.

Fast-forward to today and we're talking about self-driving cars, artificial intelligence, smart cities, 3-D metal printing, augmented reality, 5G, telemedicine, smartwatches used as medical devices, and synthetic embryos. It's hard to even fathom what we might be talking about another ten, twenty years down the road!

The net result of all this innovation is that so many of our day-to-day activities have been digitized, automated, or otherwise facilitated. Just think of how we can use technology at home. We get our news delivered to us on our smartphones in real time. We shoot off emails and text messages in seconds and are notified the moment we receive a response. We purchase gifts and groceries online and have them all delivered to our doors in a day or two. We arrange rides out to dinner with a few taps inside our Uber apps, and we can see, down to the minute, when the drivers will arrive to pick us up. It's all simple, seamless, and *instant.*

On top of reshaping how we make our buying decisions, advancements in technology have also very much reshaped our expectations when it comes to gratification.

Be honest: How long are you willing to wait for a website to load before you get annoyed and move on? A video clip? A movie you're streaming? What's a reasonable amount of time to wait for someone to respond to an email you send? To return your call? Your text message? Do you opt for online shopping instead of driving to a store and standing in line to make a purchase? What's the longest you'll wait for that order to be delivered before you reconsider that line? How much are you willing to pay in shipping fees to speed the process up?

If you have a question for someone, will you wait until the next time you see them to ask? Will you send them a message immediately? Will you bypass them altogether and see if you can find an answer online?

Again and again, research proves that we are not a patient society, and our demands for immediate turnaround are only increasing. You may have heard about Microsoft's findings: our attention spans have dropped from twelve seconds in 2000 to just over eight seconds in 2015—purportedly shorter than that of a goldfish.[4] That's why we're seeing more and more businesses harness chatbots to provide their customers with immediate feedback and support—before they inevitably point their attention elsewhere. The global chatbot market, valued at $1.17 billion in 2018, is expected to explode to over $10 billion by 2026.[5]

Google found that in addition to wanting instant responses to our inquiries, we're trending toward not even wanting to wait *one single day* before we see the results of purchases we make from our smartphones. Even tomorrow doesn't cut it anymore:

- From 2015 to 2017, travel-related searches (for hotels, plane tickets, etc.) for "tonight" and "today" increased by 150 percent.

- Over that same period, searches including "same day shipping" increased by 120 percent.[6]

And why should we wait? Why, when it's so easy, so convenient, and so affordable to get what we want precisely when we want it? We don't *have* to be patient anymore. So we aren't.

For businesses that deal in transactions, speed and convenience have become factors that will make or break their ability to succeed. That's why Amazon crossed the $1 trillion mark in September 2018.[7] And that's why smaller retailers must either find a way to keep pace or fall by the wayside.

For professional services firms, this means that if you want to attract new clients and retain the ones you already have, you *have* to stay on your toes. If a potential client perceives that you're taking too long to answer their inquiry, don't expect to get their business. If a current client perceives that you're taking too long to deliver the results they're looking for, don't expect to hear from them again, and don't be surprised if you get a not-so-glowing review from them online, which your future prospective clients *will* read (with or without a grain of salt).

Because remember: Buyers know full well how many competing firms are out there salivating for their business. All it will take is a quick search on their phones, and whichever firm gives them the best initial impression will enter the ring as your potential replacement.

The Big Picture

While the practice of law itself has remained constant at its core, the landscape within which the industry operates has, for better or for worse, undergone a complete transformation over the past couple of decades as a direct result of the whirlwind of advances in technology.

To sum it up: Clients have more power today than they ever have previously. Hyper-informed and sapped of almost all patience, they have little—if any—tolerance for sluggish responses (human or digital), inefficiencies, mediocre output, and anything less than what they perceive to be the best service their hard-earned money can buy.

This situation leaves law firms with two options:

1 Rise to the challenge and adapt to this new reality.

2 Remain stagnant as tension mounts.

In the next section, we'll look at the ways that many firms are operating within this new landscape today (spoiler: it smacks of Option #2) and the effects those ways have on their ability to work effectively, serve their clients, and ultimately succeed.

Your Law Firm, Present Day

As you read each of these snapshots, consider how it compares to your experience at your firm on a day-to-day basis. While we'll get to more systematic benchmarking a little later in this book, this anecdotal exploration will give you a basic idea of where your firm stands—and where you have opportunities to step up your game.

Identifying a Potential New Client

"Here's my next blog post for the site. Would you mind publishing it this afternoon? I'll be heading out for an event soon, but have a few prospects in mind that I want to send that article to."

"Sure thing—I'll have this up within the hour."

All this web marketing is fine and good—you can see the value in it, in becoming a trusted "thought leader" in your space. Your firm has even hired a consultant to teach you what to write about to get the most attention online and how to convert that attention into actual new clients. But all that is a long-term play. In the meantime, you get yourself out there. Your goal: to attend at least one networking event every month. Personal connections have been and always will be the key to your success. That, you are sure of.

Winning That Client's Business

It's time for another interrogation.

That's what it feels like, at least. You're heading into a meeting with a potential new client and are prepared to answer their laundry list of questions. The prospect will have done plenty of their own research in advance. You are probably one of two, three, maybe even four firms they will meet with. Most of the time, their questions center on a few main ideas:

- How likely it is that you'll get them the outcome they are looking for

- How quickly you can achieve that outcome

- What sort of fee deal you can cut for them

- How they can be sure you'll keep all of their information safe along the way

You can't blame them—with so many decent firms out there, clients are naturally going to try to find the best value for the lowest price.

Securing Repeat Business

You've dropped the ball. It has been five months since you checked in with your client—you are almost a full quarter late. It probably isn't a deal-breaker, though. At least you hope not.

You put a ton of extra effort into the last matter with this client, and you have the sense that they trust you as their advisor, not just their lawyer. They can find a lawyer anywhere. But an *advisor*...

For the past couple of years, you have been making it a practice to touch base with your clients every quarter. Seeing if there is anything you can help with. Staying top-of-mind. Making it easier for them to respond to your message than to go elsewhere. They'd be silly to go elsewhere. At least you hope so.

Catching Up on Missed Communications

Monday morning, 9:00. You're checking your phone as you wait for the Keurig to pump out your cup of coffee—the first of many. You almost don't notice your coworker approach.

"Morning! How was your weekend?"

"Oh, hey there. Busy one for me. Couple of ball games for the kids, a ton of emails, and jumped on a couple of client calls in between running errands. Lined up three calls back-to-back for this morning, starting in ten minutes, but this machine sure is taking its time!"

"I hear you. I could only squeeze in a few hours of work this weekend, so I have to hit the ground running this morning. And I will…if you ever get done brewing that cup!"

Your phone buzzes with a new email. You read the preview as you add milk and two sugar packets to your mug.

"Well, the first client on the list has asked to move the call up to, uh, right now. Guess I'll see you around!"

And with that, another whirlwind day begins.

Having a Conversation with Another Attorney

You can tell from the green indicator that Nick is at his desk and online, so you send him a direct message: *Hey, got a sec?*

The app shows that he's typing a response.

Sure. Ring my extension.

You dial his three digits, make a couple clicks in your Tabs3 software to start recording time, and get down to business.

Doing Research

You have your list of keywords at the ready. The first goes into the search bar, and within seconds you have a list of every case in the United States that relates to that keyword. You skim the summaries, identifying those that seem relevant to your case. You'll read them in full. Then you'll flip to the next keyword and repeat the process.

There are a few tricks to this process: you have to know which keywords to use, and you have to be able to extrapolate a lot of information from the summary text (it isn't always obvious which cases could be helpful, and you don't want to skip over something of real consequence for the sake of speed). But even your first-year associates got the hang of all that pretty quickly. Surprisingly quickly, as a matter of fact.

Finding a Document

Where in the world *is* this thing?!

You have searched your document management system three times now. You know what the document should be named and where it should be filed.

Should be.

You pull up your instant messenger and go straight to the source: the attorney who put that document together. (Fortunately, you know who that was, and fortunately, she is still with the firm.)

She knows the one you're talking about. It isn't in there? You're sure? Oh, it must be in her own Documents folder on her computer. She'll look for it right now; just give her a minute. Just a minute... She has her own system, you know? The firm's naming convention doesn't really make sense to her, so she uses her own. Sometime she'll show you how her files are set up—maybe her system will work well for you, too. Usually she remembers to also file the documents in the DMS, but it's an extra step and it isn't always easy to find the time. Hang tight, here it is... She'll attach it to an email and send it over to you. And since you're already in the software, would you mind popping it in there, too? She'd really appreciate it.

Collaborating on a Document

"Why can't we just set this up as a Google Doc?"

This isn't the first time a client has asked this. Google Docs, One-Drive, Dropbox—whatever file sharing system the client uses, they want you to use it as well.

"We stick to email for security reasons," you told her. Some clients accept this answer. Others keep pushing. You wonder what will happen this time.

"You don't have your own secure client portal or something that I can use? How will I be able to access all the documents we're working on?"

Nope, just email. You know it isn't the most efficient method out there—there are a bunch of versions of the file flying back and forth, and it becomes difficult to see what changes were made when, and which comments have been addressed by which person. Occasionally, two people will work on the same version at the same time, and then you have to compile their feedback into one document and send that back out to the group. It gets complicated. Most everyone in your firm is used to working that way, but more and more clients are starting to raise a fuss.

Sending and Filing a Finished Document

"Ugh, this takes *forever!*" She meant to say it under her breath, but didn't quite succeed. She makes eye contact with you, still frowning.

"I just feel like there should be an easier way to do this, you know?"

One of the five attorneys this assistant supports has just sent a finished document to a client. He converted the Word document into a PDF, slapped a digital signature on it, attached it to an email, and sent it off. And now the client has the file in hand, ahead of schedule. Great. Except…

"This one document we sent out pertains to a *dozen* different matters," she goes on. "So I have to file this in a *dozen* different places. Manually. Can't we automate this by now?"

You smile, remembering the secretaries of yesteryear hovering expectantly over their Xerox machines.

The Precarious Position of the Legal Industry

Did those snapshots resonate with you?

When we compare how a typical firm operates today versus twenty years ago, it's obvious that technology has advanced a good deal. Most firms have transitioned from paper filing systems to electronic document management systems, which (if used properly) do wonders for efficiency and security. Most attorneys can accomplish at least some of their work functions using only their smartphones, which allow them to be far more responsive to client needs. And most firms have automated enough administrative work that the number of support staff they need has drastically declined. But there's still so much to be desired.

"So what?" you might be thinking.

Really, *so what?* Things change, and it takes time to catch up. Businesses can't just turn on a dime, after all—there's risk to consider and mitigate, there's buy-in to get, there are in-depth projects to run, there are learning curves to take into account. It's a process, and a long one at that.

It does take time. It should take time. But we have to start making major, deliberate strides forward *today* for two reasons:

- **The rate of change we're experiencing is not linear, it's exponential.** The longer we wait to try to close the gap, the wider it grows, and the greater our risk of becoming completely obsolete in the meantime.

- **Law firms are notoriously resistant to change, so there's a lot more ground to cover.** If firms aren't keeping pace with other industries (which themselves lag behind), how will they fare over the next several years as the changes compound?

An Exponential Rate of Change

As Thomas Friedman puts it in *Thank You for Being Late*, we're in an "age of accelerations." The premise of his book is that since about the year 2007, the rate of technological innovation has surpassed the pace at which humans can adapt to change.

He describes the situation this way:

> ...authors, businesses, and governments basically used the same writing machine—the typewriter—for more than a century. That's three generations. That is how slow the pace of technological change was—although it was a whole lot faster than before the Industrial Revolution.[8]

Now, one generation has seen us advance from landlines to smartphones, from vinyl records to MP4s, and from VCRs to Netflix streaming on smartphones. And that generation isn't even middle-aged yet!

As innovation continues to build on innovation, we find ourselves in danger of being buried in this avalanche of change. We start hearing about things like blockchain—a technology that investors poured nearly $3.9 billion into during the first three quarters of 2018[9] and a technology that the vast majority of us hardly grasp as a concept. We know it has something to do with Bitcoin, which appears to have cycled through inception, boom, and burst in ten short years, but that's all most of us really know.

In fact, it is actually impossible for any of us to keep up, and it has been for over a decade. As Friedman writes:

> ...if it is true that it now takes us ten to fifteen years to understand a new technology and then build out new laws and reg-

ulations to safeguard society, how do we regulate when the technology has come and gone in five to seven years?[10]

A few years ago, I had a consultant survey my existing and prospective clients (specifically, a sampling of small to mid-sized law firm and association executives in the D.C. Metro area) to determine their top concerns with their organizations' technology. To my surprise, the responses came back almost unanimous: These executives experienced serious anxiety about the pace of technological change. How were they supposed to keep up and not be blindsided by all the innovation? How were they supposed to know which of these new trends were actually worth their attention (and their investment) and which were just hype? How were they supposed to keep track of what technologies others in their industries were using so that they wouldn't lag behind in comparison? As the pace continues to quicken, this anxiety will only grow. To this day, the fact that we've implemented a program to consistently educate our clients on relevant technology trends is a major differentiator for my company.

And the reality is this: We *can't* keep up with it all. But if we don't *try*, the world around us will soon enough be unrecognizable.

Industry Resistance

On a scale from Lagging to Innovative, where would you say most law firms fall?

According to Altman Weil's *2018 Law Firms in Transition Survey*, which polled 801 firms with fifty or more lawyers, the majority of firms aren't in any rush to make any big changes in the way they work: "Despite under-performance, overcapacity, financial volatility, and encroaching competition from a variety of sources, 59% of law firms say they are 'not feeling enough economic pain' to motivate more significant change in the way they deliver legal services."[11] Despite all the changes in how clients are making buying decisions, despite the sky-high expectations that active clients have for their overall experiences with their chosen law firms, and despite the obvious signs of tension between these expectations and reality (both internally and externally), the majority of law firms remain steadfast. They've done business a certain way for however many decades, and they will continue to do business that way for however many more. After all, they've made it this far, haven't they?

I understand that mindset. As my own IT industry goes through major upheaval, I still take comfort in the simplicity of the billable hour for some of the work we do. But if I don't adapt to the newer, more complex models of engagement that my clients (and prospects) are demanding, I run the risk of obsolescence—and I've seen some of my competitors go that way.

Thomas Friedman sees this resistance we feel as a natural response. Most people, he says, respond to fast-paced change by making every effort not to catch up, but to slow down:[12]

> Who can blame them? When so many things are accelerating at once, it's easy to feel like you're in a kayak in rushing white water, being carried along by the current at a faster and faster clip. In such conditions, there is an almost irresistible temptation to do the instinctive thing—but the wrong thing: stick your paddle in the water to try to slow down.

There's comfort in what is familiar, and we perceive danger in what is not. But what Thomas Friedman argues, what I argue, and what Altman Weil argues is that we'll find far greater danger in resisting the changes around us. The *Law Firms in Transition Survey* puts it this way (emphasis mine):[13]

> Longer-term challenges demand longer planning time frames. Too often law firms are myopic when thinking about changes in the way they do things. For firms to be successful in the future (not just survive), they must have an effective business

model that looks beyond short-term financial returns to support and advance long-term sustainability.

Such a business model will incorporate effective allocation of key human and technology resources and flexible, scalable operational processes that deliver both profitability and potent client value. Although most firms acquiesce to client demands, those firms that *anticipate* demands and bring innovation to their clients will be highly sustainable.

There are clear signals that some law firms are making a shift to new business models that will serve them well in the future and improve their sustainability. *Those that do not recognize the urgent need to begin the change process may ultimately be unable to catch up.*

We cannot resist this new landscape. We cannot simply *react* to it as it continues to evolve, either—not if we intend to thrive as businesses. We need to accept our new reality, and we need to slam down the gas pedal. As we'll explore in the next section, although many law firms aren't feeling enough pain to warrant a shift in their approaches, I'd wager that they haven't yet run the right calculations.

The Costs of Inaction

N ow for the hard costs. Combined, the societal shifts we've seen have redefined what it takes to:

- Build and maintain your reputation

- Attract prospective clients

- Win business away from your competitors

- Meet and exceed client expectations

- Win repeat and referral business

- Attract the best talent to your firm

- Engage and retain your employees

It follows that those firms that don't adapt properly to this new landscape will take a hit in each and every one of these areas. The firms that do adapt will excel, to the—now compounded—detriment of their less savvy competitors.

To make the case for how serious this situation actually is, let's quantify the impact that inaction could have on your firm. I'll sum the costs up in three buckets: loss of new business, loss of existing clients, and disengagement that breeds turnover.

Loss of New Business

If we don't adapt to the way our buyers are making their decisions, fewer and fewer will decide to buy from us.

Earlier I mentioned that 83 percent of people seeking attorneys will check lawyer reviews as their first step in the selection process. You may have also seen that all buyers, on average, carry out a full *67 percent of their journey* digitally.[14] This means that although your potential customers might talk to folks at your firm at different points along the way, their decisions will primarily be based on information they've found by themselves online. If that 67 percent of their journey is full of underwhelming reviews and unsubstantiated value propositions ("We're the best! Take our word for it!"), you're going to have to put some herculean effort into that remaining 33 percent to have even a modest chance of winning that business away from your more polished competitors.

And if your site isn't up to snuff on a purely technical basis, forget it. When it comes to smartphone use, Google found the following:[15]

- For every one-second delay in a website's loading, conversions can fall by over 20 percent.

- If a site takes three seconds to load, more than half of visitors will leave altogether.

Take a moment to visit testmysite.thinkwithgoogle.com. This page analyzes your mobile site's loading time and calculates the percentage of visitors who are likely to leave. What are your results? How might that visitor loss be affecting your firm's revenue, even conservatively?

It seems absurd when you think about it: Remember how long it used to take to dial up to the internet? Now most of us won't wait a measly *three seconds* for a website to load on our phones before we get so annoyed that we close out of it and move on to the next option (because there is *always* another option within reach). And one poor review from one stranger on the internet can have the same effect. These seemingly small details have a massive impact on how others will perceive your firm.

This highly digital journey is a new frontier for all of us. Those firms that choose to approach this shift as an opportunity, rather than as an unwelcome disruption to be resisted, will have the competitive edge—and the revenue to show for it.

Loss of Existing Clients

In the same way inaction can cost your firm new business, it can cost you repeat business just as easily. These days your clients aren't going to let you off the hook for a poor experience because *they don't have to*. Another conclusion from the *Law Firms in Transition Survey* (emphasis mine):[16]

> Clients want greater cost effectiveness and value—*and they are in a position to insist.* This is not new, but the recession accelerated the demand for greater efficiency and lower overall costs. Clients are clamoring for more cost-effective legal services and technology-driven process improvements. A host of alternative service providers have created a new set of lower-priced competitors for many law firms. If a firm does not provide reliably high-quality outcomes and client service at predictable, agreeable prices, *there are other providers that will.*

The "sale" is not the finish line; it's the beginning of the client's evaluation of your performance: Will you meet and exceed their expectations, thereby winning their loyalty and repeat business? Or will the experience fall flat?

As we service providers are well aware, there's no shortage of instances in which friction can wiggle its way into our relationships with our clients. In today's hyper-competitive marketplace, this friction is enough to send our clients packing, since the walk to the next provider will take only a moment. When I was conducting interviews for this book, I asked each participant what they perceived as the biggest sources of frustration for their clients. Here's what they told me:

■ Paying their attorney to perform work that could (and should, in their eyes) be automated, like searching for related case documents

- Paying their attorney for unnecessary litigation games, in which the goal appears to be racking up more billable hours rather than doing what's right for the client

- Paying their attorney for a bunch of inconsequential activities, like driving to their office for a meeting

- Not having any visibility into the progress their attorneys are making until it's time to pay the bill

- Not having a good way to collaborate on work product

- Not feeling confident that their data is safe from cyberattack

If we condense these, we're looking at complaints about bloated costs, lack of efficient service, and insufficient technical controls. Do these complaints ring true for your own clients? If not yet, could you see this sort of tension arising over the next year? Two years? Three?

Unfortunately, one bad experience with your firm is enough to discourage that client from ever working with you again; even if your current case or matter brings in revenue for your firm, the likelihood that you'll get repeat or referral business from that client is slim to none. I don't imagine these clients will leave you the most pleasant feedback on those review sites, either, and poor reviews will affect your ability to attract new business.

How heavily does your firm rely on repeat business today? On client referrals? At Optimal, the overwhelming majority of our new clients come in as referrals from our current clients. That means the stakes are that much higher when it comes to client satisfaction; if my current clients decide to leave or pare back services, then I lose not only that revenue but also my largest and most reliable source of future revenue. And that means my sales and marketing team will have to work that much harder to turn lukewarm and cold leads into closed deals. For your firm, it could mean that your attorneys spend time on business development instead of on billable work. Now you're barely treading water.

It's a nasty, expensive cycle to fall into, and one that's a real challenge to pull your firm out of. It can even be hard to identify as it's actively happening; as a prior executive coach of mine once said, "No one fires their law firm; they just start using another one." That's why it becomes so critical to position your firm ahead of these potential pitfalls and to make sure that your firm is the one that all these disgruntled clients come flocking to—not the one they're leaving.

Disengagement and Turnover

In addition to affecting your ability to attract and retain clients, sticking to the status quo will also threaten your ability to bring qualified candidates aboard and to keep the ones you do hire on the ship.

First, let's address the elephant in the room: *Millennials*. One of my clients recently told me that their young associates embody the future value of their firm. This is absolutely true, and it encapsulates what our businesses put at stake when we ignore the needs of the group that will dominate both our workforce and our client base over the coming years.

Millennials, those born between 1981 and 1996, make up more than a quarter of the United States population at 80 million strong. By 2025, they'll make up a full three-quarters of the global workforce.[17] To my fellow Gen-Xers and to you Baby Boomers: take a moment to put yourself in the shoes of the average Millennial: You've grown up your whole life with Facebook, Facebook Messenger, Snapchat, Instagram, and texting and with the collaborative features of Google Docs. You are able, within a matter of seconds, to reach your friends and your classmates by text or video chat to work on a document together, collaborate on a project, or plan an event. All of your information is organized digitally and posted online for you to access instantly if you ever need it. In other words, this culture of instant gratification is all you've ever known—it's your baseline expectation when it comes to, well, everything!

Suddenly you walk into a firm—at your first job, maybe your second job—and you're seated at a computer running Windows 7, Word, and Microsoft Outlook 2010. If you want to reach a coworker, you can send them an email, pick up the phone, or walk to their office and hope they have a moment for you. It makes no sense. It was just a quick question. Something that should have taken five seconds is now an ordeal: you save the document, compose an email message, attach the document, send it, and wait. It's a very inefficient way to work.

For Gen-Xers like me, it would be the same as if someone took away our email and our networks and made us go back to those days of working in DOS with WordPerfect 5.1, or on an IBM Selectric typing out memos and using Wite-Out. It's like sending us back in time. It's unfamiliar. It's uncomfortable. It's awkward. And worst of all, it is slow.

Millennials in this sort of situation have had to adapt their processes and slow down and work less efficiently. It makes them feel a touch powerless. It sets them back on their heels, and they start to wonder if their chosen employers are supporting them to get the job done or placing them in shackles and making it difficult for them to succeed.

Dr. Joanne Sujansky and Dr. Jan Ferri-Reed predicted this same sentiment over ten years ago, in their 2006 book, *Keeping the Millennials: Why Companies Are Losing Billions in Turnover to This Generation—and What to Do About It:* "To saddle them with antiquated technology in the workplace is to send the message that the organization is not serious about the work. After all, why wouldn't you give them the tools to do the job that you've assigned them to perform?"[18] In *What Millennials Want from Work: How to Maximize Engagement in Today's Workforce*, Jennifer Deal and Alec Levenson take this issue a step further, noting the resentment Millennials will feel as a result: "Millennials are quite aware of how much more they could get done with more efficient technology and work processes. If they feel overloaded and see a fix their organization refuses to implement, they are likely to become even more resentful of the overload."[19]

And this generation, more than any other, will leave your firm for these reasons. PricewaterhouseCoopers found that 38 percent of Millennials are actively looking to switch roles, and 43 percent are open to offers.[20] In the legal industry specifically:

- Almost half of your entry-level associates will leave within three years.

- Eighty-one percent will leave within five years.

- Recruiting and training a first-year associate costs $250,000.

- When an associate leaves, it'll cost you another $400,000.[21]

Talk about some troubling numbers. And what's worse? Although we often talk about this issue of disengagement and turnover within the context of Millennials specifically, the problem actually spans the entire workforce in a big way. A recent Gallup report took stock of how engaged today's workers are by generation. The study grouped employees into three categories of engagement, which Gallup defines as follows:

Engaged employees work with passion and feel a profound connection to their company. They drive innovation and move the organization forward.

Not-Engaged employees are essentially "checked out." They're sleepwalking through their workdays, putting time—but not energy or passion—into their work.

Actively Disengaged employees aren't just unhappy at work; they're busy acting out their unhappiness. Every day, these workers undermine what their engaged coworkers accomplish.

Their takeaway was that Millennials as a generation are the least engaged of all. But Millennials barely scrape by with the title—not a *single* generation can say they are more engaged than not.[22]

Generation	Engaged	Not Engaged	Actively Disengaged
Traditionalists	45%	41%	14%
Baby Boomers	33%	48%	19%
Gen-Xers	32%	50%	18%
Millennials	29%	55%	16%

At the macro level, disengagement in the workplace is costing our economy between $450 and $550 billion in lost productivity annually.[23] At the micro level, disengagement costs each of our businesses quite a lot, even on a day-to-day basis. In his book *Thrive by Design*, Don Rheem defines four categories of engagement based on the level of discretionary effort the individual will volunteer at work: Actively Disengaged, Disengaged, Engaged, and Actively Engaged. Here's a look at how productivity tends to play out based on each employee's engagement level:[24]

Engagement Level	Typical Portion at this Level	Days Worked per 1 Day of Pay
Actively Disengaged	5–15%	.5
Disengaged	35–50%	.67
Engaged	20–35%	1.0
Actively Engaged	5–15%	1.5

Do some quick calculations. How much, on an annual basis, could disengagement be costing your firm right now?

Final Thought

From my perspective, these three cost centers—losing new business, losing current clients, and losing or having disengaged employees—represent more than enough pain to justify a shift in how law firms are operating. What's your take? Does this information make the case for change inside your firm? As an attorney or a Firm Administrator, can you take this to your Managing Partner as a critical firm initiative? As a Managing Partner, are you convinced that mitigating these risks is worth your time and money? If so, I invite you to continue on to Part 2 of this book, where we'll construct the vision for what a wildly successful firm looks like. This is a firm that not only adapts to this new, rapidly changing landscape but uses it to their advantage. We'll explore why customer service sits at the crux of this vision and what role technology plays in realizing it.

The latter half of this book gets more complex; although the concept behind our vision is simple, the path toward achieving it is not. The shifts we've experienced over the past few decades have been nothing short of tectonic, so we're going to have to put in some work to (1) properly adapt to them, and (2) use them to our benefit. My goal is to provide you with the tools and the guidance to make this journey safely and confidently. I hope you'll join me.

PART 2

From Threat to Asset

The Linchpin: Exceptional Customer Service

It all comes down to service.

Yes, you read that correctly: I, the Tech Guy, am telling you that *service* is the solution to this predicament. Technology is no more than a tool. It will play a role in achieving the vision we create for a thriving modern law firm, but our focus must remain—at all times—on the level of service we're delivering to our clients.

As the *2018 Law Firms in Transition Survey* puts it, firms need to shift away from an internal focus and toward an external one: "Too many law firm plans focus on fixing internal issues, rather than on clients and markets. This is a mistake. Ask if executing your plans will lead to more efficient delivery of services and add value for clients."[25] The Thomson Reuters *2019 Report on the State of the Legal Market* puts similar emphasis on clients as a firm's primary focus:[26]

> As client needs, expectations and behaviors are changing, we are seeing many firms adopt highly innovative approaches to drive greater efficiency, predictability and cost-effectiveness. Clients have more choices than ever for meeting their legal needs, and leading firms are now tailoring their strategies and delivery models to provide legal services in the manner that most effectively intersects with clients' considerations.

At the end of the day, we lose prospects and clients and staff all for the same reason: misalignment between what they expect and what we deliver. This misalignment takes an infinite number of forms. A potential client expects to be able to reach you easily over the web, can't, and abandons you as an option. A current client expects to be able to collaborate with you effectively, can't, and goes elsewhere the next time they need help. These situations boil down to poor customer service, and the consequences are devastating.

The only way firms will thrive in coming years is by providing their prospective and current clients with the right experiences. The journey begins the moment people identify a problem that needs solving, takes them through their buying decision, and—depending on your field of law—continues for years to come.

As we explored in the previous section, each of the shifts we're seeing in the industry has a direct impact on how clients are interacting with your firm and what shapes their perception of a good or poor client experience. The paradigm has changed dramatically over the past couple of decades, and the intensity of this shift will continue to increase as time passes. Not only do we need to understand and internalize what this new client experience looks like from the client's perspective, but we also need to take great care to deliberately mold and nurture this experience from the outset.

One of the things that's becoming clear in this internet-driven economy is that suppliers across all industries (and employers across all industries) are replaceable. Think of it in terms of a dating service. Twenty years ago, you didn't go online to find a "match"; you had to go to the skating rink or the gym or the bar or take up some interactive hobby that got you around other people. The access to options, comparatively speaking, was limited. Today, you sign up for any of the countless online dating services or you download a dating app onto your phone. You set your search radius. You get a list of people, whom you literally swipe "yes" or "no" to after half a second of consideration. And you can do that because there are twenty, fifty, or a hundred other people lined up behind them. There are no barriers to alternatives anymore.

It's the exact same story with vendors. If I were to pop onto my LinkedIn page and take two seconds to type, "Hey, I'm looking for help with sales and marketing," I would be *deluged* with pitches. And all of those vendors would be instantly commoditized in that list of potential suppliers. On the other side of the coin, if one of my clients were to get sick of working with Optimal one day, and they knew there were fifty other IT firms out there hungry for their business—many of whom were actively cold-calling them and emailing them and otherwise banging down their door—they would be far more willing to consider a switch than if the alternatives were scarce. It just isn't the same sort of committed vendor relationship it was in the past. So either we find a way to continually bolster this loyalty, or we leave the door wide open to those who will.

Flipping the Narrative: From Threat to Advantage

Time for the good news! We aren't just talking about avoiding risks here. Yes, stagnation will result in lost clients and lost revenue and lost talent, and yes, it's critical to a firm's survival that we mitigate these risks. But more than that, we can actively flip the threat that is this shifting landscape into a competitive advantage.

Recall that the current landscape has reshaped what it takes to build and maintain your reputation, attract prospective clients, win new business, meet and exceed client expectations, win repeat and referral business, attract the best talent to your firm, and engage and retain your employees. Now imagine that your firm has committed itself to providing mind-blowing service to your clients from their very first (likely digital) interaction with your firm. Here's what that experience could look like:

1 A potential client has a need. They search online for the "best" firms in their area. Your name comes up over and over again. You're ranked highly on every review site. The prospect visits your website and can immediately sense that you just *get* what they're going through and they can trust you to solve their problem.

2 By the time you have your first interaction with a prospective client, they are basically convincing *you* to do business with *them*.

3 Given all the research your new client has done in advance of your meeting, you spend less time on administrative discussion and more time on billable work.

4 Along the way, their questions are answered promptly and accurately. You offer advice above and beyond what they are seeking. They're relieved and grateful for the guidance.

5 Collaboration with your team is quick and painless; it's almost as easy as communicating back and forth with friends and family. With all the stress they were already enduring, not having to struggle to work through a simple document is a blessing.

6 You deliver your final work product, along with a way to quantify the value that your client takes away from the interaction. They don't question the bill they receive; the investment was well worth the outcome.

7 They rave online about how fantastic their experience was with you.

8 Prospective clients, seeing these effusive reviews and the promise of measurable results, opt to look into your firm instead of similar firms in the area.

9 The process begins anew.

In the same way the internet has the potential to destroy a firm's reputation, it has just as much potential to become a weapon that's yours for the wielding. And in the same way your firm's internal technology can be a major source of angst, it can also be the method of delivering the smoothest and most pleasant experience your clients have ever encountered.

Defining "Exceptional Customer Service"

That all probably sounds great in theory, right? Yes, let's provide great customer service! That's what all of us in professional services are supposed to be doing anyway; I can't imagine that you or I would actively seek to provide terrible service and royally piss off all our clients.

But what does "Exceptional Customer Service" actually *mean*? It's a subjective term by nature and is too nebulous to hang your hat on. To make the concept more tangible and more achievable, I've broken it down into four core pillars that are specific to the kinds of business that law firms do and the kinds of clients you deal with. The pillars are:

1 **Responsiveness.** When your client has a problem, concern, or question, you address it fully, you communicate it in a way that suits your client, and you do this in a reasonable amount of time.

2 **Expertise.** You need to be able to bring your firm's collective historical expertise to bear as the situation demands. What you don't know offhand, you need to be able to track down (whether by locating old files or collaborating inside your firm) without a ton of rigmarole or recreating the wheel.

3 **Results.** You need to track and demonstrate your effectiveness as a firm in order to win repeat and referral business. Your clients (prospective and existing) need to know, in clear, quantifiable terms, what value you're bringing to the table—and know that they can't get that same value elsewhere.

4 **Innovation.** You need to anticipate and prepare for the impending trends—many of them technical—that are going to affect your firm and your clients. You need not be an expert on all things, but you need to stay alert and invest in learning enough so that neither you nor your clients get blindsided.

Mastering each of these four pillars is the key to differentiating your firm and winning new business. It's the key to turning your clients into raving fans who keep coming back, and who throw more and more clients your way. It's the key to keeping your attorneys and staff engaged with their work, not overwhelmed by the uphill battle they're fighting each day. It's the key to outpacing your competitors in this rapidly shifting landscape.

Pillar #1: Responsiveness

Responsiveness" is a term I hear day in and day out in the IT field. Managing Partners and Firm Administrators come to me positively fuming because their providers can't seem to deliver responsive support to their attorneys; the support folks just aren't grasping the fact that every lost minute equates to lost revenue. When we survey our clients to uncover any areas where we might be able to improve, one of the first items we'll ask them to rate is our responsiveness. In my world, responsiveness generally equates to timeliness—if your technology breaks, you want someone looking at it right away and solving the problem (or at least providing a workaround while they tackle the root of the issue) as quickly as possible so that you can get back to work.

This term takes on a slightly different meaning for law firms. In a nutshell, being responsive means bridging that aggravating gap between how easily we can communicate in our personal lives and how complicated and slow everything feels once we step into the business world. There's an aspect of efficiency here, and of having the agility to serve your clients when and how they need you to.

Efficiency

The first piece of responsiveness is being efficient in your service delivery. Your clients don't want to wait any longer than necessary for you to answer their questions or deliver your work product, and they don't want to pay a dollar more for your time than they feel they should have to (or that they would have to elsewhere for an equivalent output). Seth Berenzweig discusses efficiency as a key to staying competitive:[27]

> When you're working on deals and drafts and litigation work product, your client can see when you don't have the technology and supporting staff to deploy the resources you need for a case. In large-scale litigation cases, you can have tens of thousands of documents you're dealing with. If you can't do a keyword search in minutes and are doing an old-school manual search over the course of *days*, you're out.

Roy Niedermayer has a similar take: If it's taking your firm a hundred hours to complete a task another firm can finish in ten, thanks to better technologies or better staffing, you can't compete. Your costs will be bloated, and your service will be, comparatively speaking, poor.[28]

Thomson Reuters' *2017 Report on the State of the Legal Market* notes how client behavior is being shaped more and more by the desire for efficient and cost-effective service:[29]

> …clients over the past 10 years have been increasingly willing to break particular matters into their constituent parts and to decide, with respect to each part, how the services needed could be provided most efficiently and cost-effectively. Sometimes this has resulted in clients moving certain functions in-house, sometimes in outsourcing certain functions to legal process outsourcers or other non-law firm vendors, and sometimes in moving certain functions to other lower-cost law firms.

In fact, efficiency was one of two core differentiators between firms that remained stagnant and those that excelled; the *2017 Dynamic Law Firms Study* found that although growth in the market has been "flat to neutral" since the Recession of 2008, firms outperformed their competitors by a long shot when they invested in technology that allowed them to (a) increase efficiencies via automation, and (b) collect and evaluate data on profitability. The *2018 Report on the State of the Legal Market* reaffirms this need for efficiency, predictability, and cost-effectiveness, and it views the results of the *2017 Law Firms in Transition Survey* as evidence that firms are taking note and adapting their operations accordingly in order to remain competitive:[30]

- Fifty percent of the nearly four hundred firms surveyed have significantly changed their staffing strategies since the Recession.

- Forty-nine percent have significantly changed their approaches to enhancing efficiency in the delivery of legal services.

- Thirty-nine percent have made significant changes in their pricing models.

- Forty-nine percent are using technology to replace human resources with the aim of improving efficiencies.

Now, when it comes to the debate over hourly billing and shifting your firm toward more alternative fee arrangements that encourage greater efficiency, I make no pretense of analyzing the issue from any perspective other than that of your clients: the quicker you get me what I need, the happier I am, and the more likely I am to come back with return business, to leave positive reviews online, and to tell my friends and colleagues about you.

The pressure to deliver high-quality work faster and at a reasonable cost is especially heavy in light of sites like LegalZoom. Potential clients, turned off by the prospect of investing so much time and money in legal services, can easily abandon the whole idea of vetting and hiring a lawyer, and instead use an online service to draw up the documents they need in next to no time flat and for a fraction of a fraction of the cost. That, or they can visit their local courthouse's website, navigate to the self-help or e-services section, download forms, and file the forms themselves.

Frank Schipani, Director of IT and Operations at Three Crowns LLP and past President of the ALA Capital Chapter, makes an important point: getting work done faster *doesn't mean there's less work to go around.* In fact, increasing efficiencies might mean that your firm is able to take on a case or matter you wouldn't have the opportunity to pursue otherwise. At that point, not only are your clients happier, but your efficiency is now literally generating more work for your firm.[31]

Agility and Flexibility

The other side of responsiveness is being available to your clients whenever (and wherever) the need arises. I'll preface this section by saying that *the point is not that attorneys have to be available 24/7/365 in order to provide responsive service.* You can be if you'd like, but that decision is up to you the individual, or to "you" the collective firm. Instead, my point is that you need to have the option. If you cannot address client needs unless you are physically seated at your desk in your office, you are powerless to determine whether you want (or do not want) to take action.

Say you're sitting at home and your client calls your work number. They're in the middle of an employment negotiation with one of their key employees. They've assembled all of the important players there and didn't think they were going to need legal advice at this juncture, but as the conversation developed, they realized they need your help, and they need it now. If you're at home, are you going to know your work line is ringing, or will this request simply go unnoticed until the next morning? If you can receive the call, are you going to know it is your client and be able to take the call, begin tracking your time, and join the conversation for the next thirty minutes?

Or say you're waiting in line at the grocery store and you get an email from a client who wants to chat about a contract you've drafted for them.

You know they have a negotiation in two weeks, so you'll need to talk with them this week if you want to nail things down in time. Can you get a call on your calendar? How much effort does it take? If you aren't available, can you check to see if your partner or associate is free to take care of the matter? Can you marshal the resources at your disposal to provide service without physically being seated at your desk? Or will your inability to accommodate this request put your client's big deal at risk (and put your relationship with that client in an even more perilous position)?

Again, the boundaries between your work life and your home life are yours to set. But if you don't have the capability to blur these lines, that decision is out of your hands. And in today's landscape, that's a risk your firm may not want to take.

I am particularly taken with the perspective of Michael Gottlieb, founder of Momentum Law Group, on what it takes to provide responsive service to clients. The key, he says, is to make a concerted effort to meet the client halfway and to take into account the solutions and strategies *they're* using to communicate and collaborate at home or at their businesses.[32] How does your method interface with theirs? Should it? How? Can you make those connections without sacrificing the security of your privileged client data?

Some of my clients, for example, are using a program called Slack for their internal communications. For one client in particular, Slack is *so deeply ingrained* into their operations and their culture that some folks would rather have their technology issues go unresolved than to go outside of this central hub and call us, email us, or submit a support ticket to us through our online portal. Since we're also using Slack at Optimal, since we already offer Slack implementation services to our clients, and since my folks always love a new challenge, we've built a method for this client to submit and interact with their support tickets through Slack. It's not a particularly drastic, risky, or costly leap for us, and it has the potential to take our relationship with that client to an entirely new level—one they aren't likely to achieve with another provider in our space. You have this same sort of opportunity inside your firm.

Finally, you need to take into account how you're delivering your final work product. Are you using email to send documents back and forth? Do you have a portal where clients can access their documents on demand? Does your website have a self-service page where clients can download standard forms? Do clients have their own file sharing solutions that are secure enough for you to tap into? (Tip: Many consumer solutions are not.)

The more seamless an experience you can offer your clients, and the less effort they have to put in on their end to work with you—from start to finish—the more thrilled they're going to be with your service.

Exceptional Customer Service			
Responsiveness	Expertise	Results	Innovation

Pillar #2: Expertise

It is, of course, critical for any firm to have the required legal competence in order to properly serve its clients. I'd imagine that your firm wouldn't have made it very far if you didn't have a team of capable, qualified, intelligent attorneys on your bench. This isn't the kind of expertise I'm talking about. Your team's knowing your particular area of law cold is a given, in the same way it's a given that my engineers know computer networking cold. Big deal. That's why they're called "lawyers" and "engineers" to begin with. Those are table stakes.

When it comes to providing your clients with Exceptional Customer Service, expertise means going beyond basic legal know-how. It means taking a strategic—not just tactical—approach to your services and guiding your clients through tough decisions. It means being able to bring your entire firm's worth of knowledge and experience to bear for your clients' benefit. It means giving them more value than they'd ever be able to find by themselves online.

Strategic Mindset

On top of knowing the law, firms that intend to remain competitive must be able to translate the law for their clients and provide intelligent, thoughtful, strategic advice based on the implications of that law. Seth Berenzweig sees this strategic element as crucial to providing Exceptional Customer Service:[33]

> Clients want a firm that can sit down with them and answer
> legal problems today, but also ... help them formulate strat-

egies that help them grow tomorrow. We can't just be an encyclopedia; we have to be an advisor. If you can have that conversation with your clients, and become a confidant, you're in for the long-term. Otherwise you're just a fire hydrant.

Now, fire hydrants have their place—a client has an emergency, and they need your help dousing the flames. Your firm needs to be able to do this. My company needs to be able to do this, too, as technology has a special way of, well, breaking. But if that's the full scope of our capabilities, we will be seen as commodities.

Take contract writing, for example. All of my clients sign multi-year service agreements. This document serves as the basis for our partnership and sets the guidelines and the tone for the years ahead. If I engage with your firm to craft this contract for me, you can deliver a product that checks all the legal boxes, keeps my company protected, gives my clients crystal-clear expectations, and stands up to any litigation that could arise from disputes. That's fine. Or you can give me a contract that functions as an extension of my sales process and my culture and makes my prospective clients all the more likely to add their signatures without a long, drawn-out (and potentially deal-breaking) negotiation process. How?

- Instead of functioning as a one-sided legal document, the agreement takes my client's needs and fears into account and seeks to make clients comfortable with what is often a high-stakes, high-stress transition.

- The contract explicitly states what we expect from our clients and what they can expect from us. No games, no secrets.

- The language itself aligns with the messaging the client has seen throughout the rest of the sales process—they aren't suddenly slapped with a bunch of dense jargon that is jarringly different from every interaction they've had with my company so far.

- Each and every section of the contract has been evaluated from the client's perspective, and all potentially confusing or off-putting words, phrases, or sections have been flagged, discussed, revised, reevaluated, and *then* finalized.

With that kind of contract, you're not just taking the law into account. You're taking my business into account. You're taking my sales process into account. You're taking my personal philosophies into account. You're taking the psychology of my clients into account. So long as you don't put me through a hellish collaboration process to put a document like that together, I will go out of my way to give you my business and to send any of my friends or business partners your way if they ever have a similar need.

That's the sort of approach that the most successful firms will take. It's one thing to part ways with a lawyer. It's quite another to part ways with a trusted advisor.

Breadth

Your (reasonable) clients are not going to expect each individual at your firm to memorize every single bit of the entire practice's historical information. They are, however, going to expect that you can search for, locate, and use that information without much ado, and not have to spend your time and their money duplicating efforts. In other words, you need to be in the position to capture and leverage your firm's collective expertise. One of the fundamental benefits of outsourcing, after all, is that you gain access to a team of expert resources, all of whom have varying amounts of experience and historical work product to offer. Clients choose to engage with my firm rather than hiring an internal IT Director because they want more knowledge, experience, perspective, and scale than could possibly be contained in one person. Clients choose to engage with your firm rather than relying on internal legal counsel or a solo practitioner for the same reason. So if you aren't able to bring all of this information to bear in an effective way, why is your client outsourcing in the first place?

One aspect of leveraging your firm's expertise is being able to pull in the right human resources at the right time to deliver the right results to your clients. Here's an example: I work with several clients who are subject to HIPAA compliance regulations. All of their vendors, including my company, must sign a Business Associate Agreement (BAA), which essentially states that my people are also responsible for keeping this Protected Health Information secure. Recently, a client sent me one of these agreements, which I emailed to my lawyer, who then forwarded it to a junior associate who had experience with HIPAA. This associate reviewed the document and sent it back to me with her feedback in next to no time. I got all the information I needed more quickly and at a lower rate than if the request had been fulfilled by my lawyer. Those are the results I outsource for.

Another example: If one of my network engineers notices that a client's time-and-billing software is causing firm-wide angst, wasted time, and missed billings, they can suggest an in-depth evaluation and needs assessment. When the assessment is complete, they can ask the client's assigned Client Success Manager to speak with firm leadership and determine if the impact is meaningful enough to warrant an additional investment. If it is, we can bring our CIO consultants in to manage that software selection project from start to finish. Those are the results my clients are outsourcing for.

Besides being able to call upon your firm's human resources, you need to be able to access its digital resources. As I talk to law firms about the challenges they're facing with their technology, having to repeatedly re-create documents is one that I hear over and over again. A client needs a deliverable that you *know* someone at the firm has created before, but you can't locate that file because of one of the following situations:

- It lives on that one attorney's machine and nowhere else (and should they ever leave the firm, they'll take all that data with them).

- It's stored somewhere that you can theoretically access, but you have no clue where, and the only way to search for it is through a brutal manual process that isn't even worth the effort.

- You have one centralized, indexed, fully searchable document management system in place, but one of the partners never really took to it and still files her documents elsewhere, other partners don't quite follow the naming conventions, and some partners aren't really sure how to use the platform, so you can't trust what the searches pull out for you.

- You have an effective, robust document management solution in place that the entire firm has adopted, but you can access it only from your physical office, which is inaccessible due to snow, road closures, or what-have-you.

So the attorney builds the document from scratch (perhaps overlooking an important aspect that the original document would have brought to their attention), taking far more time than should be necessary (which aggravates both the attorney and the client) and resulting in a much higher bill for your client (which aggravates them even more). Not only is this inefficient, but it cheats your client out of much of the value of outsourcing.

To achieve the level of breadth that your clients expect and deserve, you must eliminate the barriers—technical, procedural, or cultural—between them and all the knowledge your firm has accumulated over time. This, combined with a strategic mindset, results in the kind of value that your clients won't easily find elsewhere.

Pillar #3: Results

C lients—both prospective and existing—want to see results. This is true for every investment that anyone makes at any time: *Did I get what I wanted out of this purchase?* This is especially true in legal services, where the price tags can be particularly overwhelming to the average client; they need to see the value to justify these large expenses.

Enter: Results. I'm talking about the tangible, concrete, measurable value that your firm and your attorneys are providing and that is visible to the outside world. These results quantify your success with your current clients and communicate those successes to your prospective clients.

The *2018 Law Firms in Transition Survey* found that only half of firms are able to clearly communicate their value: "When asked if their law firm projects a distinct and compelling value that differentiates them from other similar firms, a full 50% of firm leaders said no. In a market characterized by intense competition for limited and shrinking demand, this lack of differentiation can be an enormous problem."

A powerful way to communicate your value is to take stock of your client relationships in a more quantitative way. This is missing from the legal world in the same way it's missing from the technology world. Both of us are involved in essential business processes for our clients, yet we don't take the time to actually get our hands around the impact we're making on those processes. We could claim that we increase our clients' effectiveness, but how do we actually know if that's true? If it is, how much is the increase? Ever so slight? An order of magnitude? If you help your clients with HR matters, for example, can you measure changes in their retention rates based on work that you've done? Or maybe it would be more appropriate to measure changes in the amount of litigation your client is subject to based on steps you've taken to protect them.

Take some inspiration from that same report (all emphasis is mine):[34]

> Why should clients hire you? In a flat-demand market, where there is not enough work to go around, you must have a compelling answer. The ability to differentiate your firm from similar competing firms is fundamental.
>
> Law firms can differentiate in one or more of the following areas: *practice range, industry expertise, geographic footprint, best-in-class quality, cost/price value, service delivery and client relationship management.* Any firm or practice group can decide to differentiate themselves in one or more of these ways. Today, service delivery (efficiency) and cost/price (the client value proposition) are clearly what clients are focused on. Achievement of true differentiation typically requires a change, doing some things differently, *pursuing innovation aggressively and putting client needs first.*
>
> Every firm must define and demonstrate what makes it different and better than competitors. Firms that can develop a clear, easily-communicated, client-facing brand or message built upon one or more true differentiators will enjoy powerful competitive advantage. Client response will tell you whether you have it right.

Which of those differentiators would make the most sense for your firm? How can you quantify the value you offer in a way that will resonate with potential and current clients?

Let's go back to the example of contracts for a moment. Imagine that a prospective client is considering hiring you to help draw up their service agreements, and you are able to (honestly) tell them that you have a 100 percent win rate on collections for the contracts you've written. Would that make them more likely to sign on with you? Absolutely! (And here's the thing: your competitors might be able to claim the very same win rate, but if they aren't tracking and communicating those results, you still have the upper hand.)

Now imagine that you're able to tell that same prospective client that after you drew up new contracts for a client similar to them in size and industry, their signature rate increased by X percent and their time in negotiations decreased by Y percent, or the equivalent of $X. You have hard numbers to back up the strategic value your firm has to offer, and that is even *more* likely to elevate you above your competitors.

Then, when you've landed this new client and completed work for them, you tabulate *their* results. In many cases, they'll take that value and communicate it to the other stakeholders. They feel good about their investment, they look good to their peers, and you look good to potential new clients. Win-win-win.

This isn't a complicated notion, but it's one that few firms are acting on, and one that is perhaps the most directly influential when it comes to attracting and retaining clients.

Exceptional Customer Service			
Responsiveness	Expertise	Results	Innovation

Pillar #4: Innovation

The fourth and final pillar is what I'll call "innovation." This will likely be the most challenging pillar for your firm to embrace wholeheartedly, but it's one that promises to be a potent differentiator if you do.

Innovation, as I define it, is the habit of being on the lookout for new trends that might affect your firm and your clients and facing them head-on. It's a mindset of courage and adaptability and curiosity. And it's a mindset that is decidedly not natural for most law firms.

To provide your clients with Exceptional Customer Service, you cannot continue to lag behind the times as law firms have historically done. Instead, you need to stand at the forefront when it comes to:

1 **Using new technologies to continually improve your firm's capabilities.** There will always be new trends, like better collaboration, better communication, better tracking of cases and matters, and easier ways to track time. There may even be practical applications for artificial intelligence (AI). You can't jump on all of these at once, but you should stay alert for internal challenges that these technological improvements might address.

2 **Guiding your clients through the legal ramifications of those new technologies.** Can you, for example, represent disenfranchised employees who have been replaced by AI? Help someone with a dispute over a "smart contract" powered by blockchain technology? If you aren't familiar with the technologies

actively affecting those you serve, how well can you really serve them?

Without this final pillar in place, your firm can still perform well. You'll address your clients' needs fully and efficiently, and clients will have no question as to what sort of tangible value they're getting out of their relationships with you. But meanwhile, the landscape around you will continue to evolve ever more quickly and ever more dramatically. As your team has their heads down, working day in and day out to make your clients as happy as can be, there's a whirlwind of transformation spinning right outside your door. What are the chances that you'll get blindsided at some point? That your clients will get blindsided?

Let's return once again to Thomas Friedman and *Thank You for Being Late:* We have to keep paddling if we want to remain stable amidst the rapids.

And it's not just about avoiding negative outcomes; there's a mountain of opportunity in innovation. Some of the more nascent technology trends, such as AI and blockchain, could potentially serve as new, high-growth practice areas for your firm. If you set aside the time to do the research, and if you pull in the right legal and technical experts, in three years' time you'll be able to apply that specialized knowledge and bring in a whole new subset of clients to delight with Exceptional Customer Service.

Just think of the types of results you could measure then.

Technology
as the Primary Vehicle

Exceptional Customer Service is our goal. Technology is our vehicle.
As you might expect, technology's starring role in disrupting our landscape means that *how we choose to view and leverage technology within our business will directly impact our ability to thrive in this new environment.* If technology stands as something to be feared, ignored, or otherwise deprioritized, the gap between how your firm operates and what your clients and employees expect will only grow wider and wider until it is simply unsustainable. If technology stands as something to be valued, understood, and invested in, you can not only meet people's expectations, but exceed them.

I've spent nearly three decades in law firm technology, and I've seen overwhelming evidence of small firms' successfully leveraging technology to achieve meaningful business results. Years back, when only the military had the privilege of using GPS technology, the notion—from the client's perspective—was that the bigger the firm, the better. Large firms had the budgets for the most talented people, the most robust technical capabilities, the tightest security, and ultimately the best results with the least amount of risk on the part of the client. But today, when we're all carrying mainframes in our literal pockets, our figurative pockets need not be nearly as deep to accomplish the same goals; as advanced technology has become more accessible and more economical, we're seeing a leveling of the playing field.

Michael Gottlieb, founder of Momentum Law Group, recalls the massive amount of time, effort, and money it took his previous firm to build and maintain their technology environment twenty years ago. There were servers upon servers upon servers, tape backups to swap and store, desktop computers in each office, and a rotation of support staff to come in and manually support each and every piece of the puzzle. Fifteen years later, he was able to found his small firm with a few subscriptions to cloud applications, and he was able to create a website that's just as good as the one a firm much, much larger than his has built. In other words, from a purely technological perspective, pretty much anyone can start their own firm, be sufficiently functional, and achieve that sophisticated online presence that is so important to business development today.[35]

Bigger firms can, of course, still invest more resources in their technology and derive significant results from those investments. eDiscovery, for example, is still a very expensive technological proposition, even with the cloud services available today. But advances in technology have empowered small firms to accomplish goals they could only *dream* of a decade ago. Besides building an impressive online presence like Michael did, small firms can leverage technology to:

- Compete for and win clients with sensitive security needs.

- Expand their geographical reach with minimal effort.

- Expand their talent pool with similar ease.

- Boost morale and retention with flexible work environments.

- Save millions of dollars in rent by embracing remote work.

- And on and on.

The means to achieve powerful business results are at our fingertips. Many firms are already capitalizing on this fact.

Yours can do the same, but better.

We're not just setting out to use technology to your material benefit; that will help your firm *survive* in this new landscape, but it won't help you thrive. If your firm intends to see a wildly successful future, your charge is to deliberately and methodically harness technology to realize its vision of Exceptional Customer Service. Shift your focus outward and on to each of the four pillars as your clients experience them. Work backward from your intended results to the technology and the strategies that will allow you to achieve them. Build, maintain, and grow a base of positively delighted clients, and leave your competitors in the dust.

PART 3

Building the Foundation

Pouring the Concrete

T o extend the metaphor, you can't erect any pillars until you've first built a solid foundation.

Leveraging technology to fuel our vision of Exceptional Customer Service is an advanced application of that tool. If your firm is in a place where you don't yet use technology to manage, say, your documents, there's going to be some groundwork to do before more complex initiatives (like the ones we'll explore in the next section) are feasible from a practical, technical, or cultural perspective. So we need to get a clear baseline reading for where your firm stands today and then determine what you need to do to fill in any critical foundational gaps.

To do this, I've designed a fourteen-point model that breaks the world of technology into bite-sized chunks. I call it the Technology Operational Maturity Model[36] (T-OML for short) and have crafted it to apply to small and medium-sized law firms specifically.

When these traits are taken all together, we're looking to figure out how operationally mature your firm is when it comes to technology. There are just three levels of maturity: low (1), medium (2), and high (3). Firms that have reached medium to high T-OML for each of the fourteen traits are the firms that are best positioned to shift their focus toward harnessing technology to increase their competitive advantage. Firms that exhibit low maturity in any of these foundational areas will need to make some changes before our vision is within reach.

To move us from theory to application, I've condensed the full T-OML Assessment we perform for our clients down to a self-assessment that you can complete in this book. What has become very clear in the years I've been working in technology is how a firm looks and feels when it operates at the top levels of maturity. This is the picture I'm going to paint

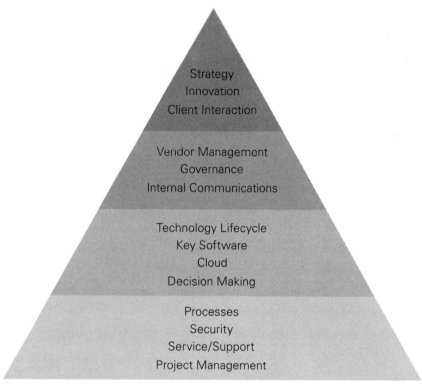

Technology Operational Maturity Model: Core Traits to Evaluate

for you in the assessment. I'll show you the main characteristics of a high-T-OML firm for each of the traits, and your job is to run through each characteristic and see if it resonates as something your firm is doing now.

As you work your way through the assessment, try not to dwell on your answers; your gut instinct is perfect. The scoring will also be pretty easy, and at the end we'll have a reasonable baseline for your firm.

Now grab a pencil, and let's get started!

Technology OML Self-Assessment

PROCESSES	
Core Concept	*How smooth are your routine IT processes?*
Highly Mature Response	☐ We have documented IT processes to keep our systems secure and running well. ☐ Our processes include daily, weekly, and monthly checklists that are followed by our IT team. ☐ We have clear technology standards that are driven by our IT strategy. ☐ We've invested in centralized management of our IT infrastructure (e.g., server monitoring, workstation patching, etc.). ☐ We have clear onboarding and offboarding procedures. ☐ New attorneys and staff are fully functional the day they walk through the door, and properly terminated the moment they leave.

Your Firm Exhibits...	① None of these	② Some of these	③ All of these

SECURITY			
Core Concept	*How well does your firm execute on security needs?*		
Highly Mature Response	❒ Our CIO (internal or external) has full ownership of the firm's security protocol and reports regularly to our Managing Partner and Firm Administrator. ❒ We have specific IT security policies in place to cover all elements of our internal security and the privacy of our client data. ❒ We have a clear, tested disaster recovery plan. ❒ We have a written business continuity plan. ❒ We have all standard technical defenses in place (and monitored), including a business-level firewall, malware protection, centralized patching, backups, and a spam filter. ❒ We've also implemented more advanced defenses, such as VPNs, laptop encryption, advanced endpoint protection, and periodic security risk assessments with remediation plans. ❒ We are able to articulate our security and data handling policies in response to external audits without consternation.		
Your Firm Exhibits…	① None of these	② Some of these	③ All of these

SERVICE/SUPPORT			
Core Concept	*How well are your attorneys and staff supported in their daily work?*		
Highly Mature Response	❏ There is a 24/7 helpdesk that we can call or email for help. ❏ Our computer issues are tracked and visible in a centralized ticketing system. ❏ There are clear targets for what type of support response is expected and when. ❏ Complex issues can immediately be escalated to higher-level support personnel for a resolution. ❏ All attorneys and staff are treated as "clients" by the IT staff, whose performance is then measured on client satisfaction.		
Your Firm Exhibits...	① None of these	② Some of these	③ All of these

PROJECT MANAGEMENT			
Core Concept	*How effective are your upgrade and implementation projects?*		
Highly Mature Response	❏ Each project is planned out well in advance. ❏ Every project has specific success criteria that are measured as part of the project review process. ❏ Firm downtime is always minimized to maximize our billing. ❏ Follow-up support is scheduled in advance. ❏ We plan clear communications, demonstrations, and training for any new technology or upgrades that will be implemented during the project. ❏ Firm leadership helps set the example on technology adoption.		
Your Firm Exhibits...	① None of these	② Some of these	③ All of these

TECHNOLOGY LIFECYCLE		
Core Concept	*Is your technology lifecycle aligned with your firm's needs?*	
Highly Mature Response	❑ We have a proactive hardware and software refresh cycle that is not dictated by performance issues or by manufacturers ending support. ❑ We plan these upgrades into our IT budget cycle. ❑ We evaluate each release of our mission-critical software for important features that would enhance our productivity or ability to serve clients. ❑ We stay informed about new software that could replace our current software to provide better features.	
Your Firm Exhibits...	① None of these	② Some of these	③ All of these

KEY SOFTWARE			
Core Concept	*How well does your firm use key software to its advantage?*		
Highly Mature Response	❏ We have a document management system (DMS), a case management system, a time-and-billing platform, and an eDiscovery package as appropriate. ❏ All of our documents (and all versions of them) are stored in the DMS, and we can find important information in seconds. ❏ We use email, but only to send links to those documents inside the DMS. ❏ All key software is used and understood by everyone in the firm—even the partners.		
Your Firm Exhibits...	① None of these	② Some of these	③ All of these

CLOUD			
Core Concept	*How easily can you scale your operations?*		
Highly Mature Response	❒ Our firm has accepted the cloud as a core part of its IT strategy. ❒ We back up our data to the cloud. ❒ All of our line-of-business applications, including document management and time-and-billing, are in the cloud (public or private). ❒ We have very clear policies on what is and is not allowed as far as additional cloud applications. ❒ We have paid attention to the security of our data as it pertains to the cloud, and we have properly vetted all of our cloud's vendors and partners against those policies. ❒ We can easily add people without adding to our internal infrastructure. ❒ Our attorneys and staff can work from anywhere as if they were in the office.		
Your Firm Exhibits...	① None of these	② Some of these	③ All of these

DECISION MAKING			
Core Concept	*To what extent are technology decisions aligned with firm strategy and needs?*		
Highly Mature Response	❑ We have specific, weighted criteria for each important IT decision as it relates to the overall firm strategy and underlying IT strategy. ❑ We collect various options from comparable firms. ❑ We take guidance from outside consultants as appropriate. ❑ Our CIO recommends solutions to us. ❑ High-dollar decisions are made by our CIO, Firm Administrator, and Managing Partner together.		
Your Firm Exhibits...	① None of these	② Some of these	③ All of these

VENDOR MANAGEMENT			
Core Concept	*How well do you utilize outside expertise and services?*		
Highly Mature Response	☐ We seek vendor recommendations from comparable firms and make our selection from there. ☐ We have specific selection criteria that are strategic, cultural, and tactical. ☐ We engage our vendors with deep multi-year relationships based on specific service levels and business outcomes. ☐ We manage these relationships at multiple levels within the firm.		
Your Firm Exhibits...	① None of these	② Some of these	③ All of these

GOVERNANCE		
Core Concept	*To what level is your IT overseen?*	
Highly Mature Response	☐ Our IT is run by a CIO-level individual (internal or external). ☐ Every person and vendor involved in IT has a clear role, understands how their role fits into the larger picture, and has clear performance expectations. ☐ We have a Technology Committee. ☐ Our Technology Committee meets on a regular basis to discuss all manner of IT issues. ☐ We have regular IT operational reviews. ☐ We are well aware of the regulations we must comply with. ☐ We execute specific and clear plans to make sure we remain in compliance.	
Your Firm Exhibits...	① None of these	② Some of these	③ All of these

INTERNAL COMMUNICATIONS			
Core Concept	*How deep and effective are your internal communications about technology?*		
Highly Mature Response	☐ We have a set IT Onboarding Agenda that we follow and present to every new hire. ☐ Every project that is implemented in the firm has some training associated with it. ☐ Our Technology Committee is charged with talking about technology initiatives with their respective groups. ☐ We have a formal Security Awareness Training program. ☐ Internal communications take place by phone, video conference, email, and instant messaging or in collaborative applications.		
Your Firm Exhibits...	① None of these	② Some of these	③ All of these

STRATEGY			
Core Concept	*To what extent is your IT strategy tied to your firm's business strategy?*		
Highly Mature Response	❑ IT is seen as more than a cost center to be minimized. ❑ Our IT strategy is directly tied to the firm's business strategy. ❑ The IT budget is highly predictable with almost no surprises. ❑ We account for growth or decline in the firm's headcount in advance.		
Your Firm Exhibits...	① None of these	② Some of these	③ All of these

INNOVATION			
Core Concept	*To what extent do you embrace and encourage technological innovation?*		
Highly Mature Response	❐ Implementation of new technologies is a regular topic at the Technology Committee meetings. ❐ There is a formal mechanism for anyone in the firm to submit technology improvement ideas. ❐ Our IT team is in regular contact with consultants and colleagues at other firms, and members attend conferences to learn about the state of technology for law firms and the innovative improvements they should be planning over the next two to three years.		
Your Firm Exhibits…	① None of these	② Some of these	③ All of these

CLIENT INTERACTION			
Core Concept	*How well do you use technology to interact with your clients?*		
Highly Mature Response	❑ We interact with our clients over the phone, by video, and via email. ❑ Each client has their own document repository, where they can access the documents we have created for them, as well as provide comments and collaborate on any document that we are working on together. ❑ We have figured out how to text and instant-message with our clients while preserving the chains of communication as needed for regulatory compliance.		
Your Firm Exhibits...	① None of these	② Some of these	③ All of these

Your Maturity Level (Total Score/14): _____

Today's Date: _____

Devising Your Roadmap

Does your Technology Operational Maturity Level align with your expectations?

Hopefully that exercise helped to put your firm's approach to technology in context and shed light on specific areas that might not be getting the right kind of attention. In addition to providing your baseline, this self-assessment also serves as a checklist for climbing higher in your overall maturity level. Here's what to do with your results.

Note What You're Doing Well

If you scored medium (2) to high (3) on some of these traits, congratulations! Take a moment to acknowledge your success, and don't you dare take your foot off of that gas pedal. I've always believed that casting our strengths aside in pursuit of improving weaknesses is foolish; if you're doing something well, *make sure you keep doing it.*

Work Your Way Up the Pyramid

Address the T-OML traits one section at a time, starting at the bottom of the pyramid.

For the first four traits—Processes, Security, Service/Support, and Project Management—which ones did you score low in? Focus on elevating your T-OML for those traits. Use the self-assessment to envision what success looks like for each trait; then determine what steps need to be taken, by whom, for your firm to get there. When you've reached medium to high maturity for every trait in that section, move up to the next batch.

If it isn't obvious to you how to make progress toward raising your maturity level in any of these areas, consider hiring a consultant to help guide the process and to assume some of the burden. There are tons of

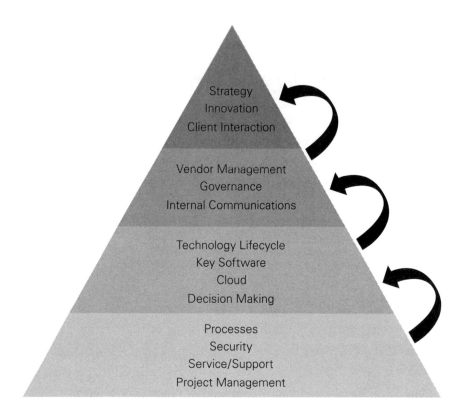

competent providers out there, especially here in the D.C. Metro area. You don't have to go it alone.

Perfect Is the Enemy of Good Enough

Remember what we're trying to do here: In order to reasonably make progress toward providing Exceptional Customer Service, your firm needs to reach *medium* maturity for each trait in the assessment. Medium maturity overall indicates that your firm places sufficient value on technology, has the management of your technology operation under enough control to effect change, and is already employing various technology tools for business gains (e.g., increased morale or increased revenue). This is the kind of footing you need before the pillars are within your grasp.

Striving to become a highly mature firm across the board is, of course, a fantastic and worthwhile long-term goal. At that point, you can start considering high-level initiatives like AI and machine learning, chatbots, and full-service client portals. But putting our vision on the back burner until you reach that point is unnecessary and, frankly, a mistake. We don't have that kind of time. Instead, we need to designate medium maturity as our jump-off point and pursue the related but discrete initiatives of Exceptional Customer Service and high maturity in parallel.

So if you fall below medium maturity today, this section can serve as your first set of marching orders. Part 4 will spell out what's to come after you hit this first milestone.

If you're already there, excellent! Give yourself a pat on the back, note where you have the opportunity to improve, and buckle up for the start of Round 2.

PART 4

Realizing the Vision

Elevating Technology's Role

I said it before, I'm saying it now, and I'll probably say it again: *Technology is a tool.*

There are two sides to that coin. The first is that technology for technology's sake is worthless; it is the means, not the end. The second is that if you wield this tool properly, the impact can be nothing short of revolutionary.

The previous section was your basic instruction manual, identifying the different parts of the tool, explaining how it works and how to care for it, and describing its standard real-world applications. With that foundational literacy in place, we can advance to the fun stuff. Be aware, though, that your firm has to be ready for it from a cultural perspective.

For most firms, this journey toward providing Exceptional Customer Service will require the implementation and adoption of a large number of new technologies, and more change in less time than you've seen perhaps ever before. So beyond getting buy-in for individual technology solutions by way of proper education and training, you're going to need the same level of buy-in for this more dynamic, forward-thinking, leading-edge technology strategy as a whole. In other words, your team has to embrace *a culture of open-mindedness* to new solutions and to new ways of doing business that adapt with the times.

Beyond the required open-mindedness, consider that many of these technologies are going to connect the individuals in your firm in a way they haven't been connected before. As you build a more communicative, collaborative, transparent digital workspace, your people have to grow comfortable with shifting their mindsets from "me and my practice" to "us and our practice."

In my experience, firms that are on the cusp of some seriously positive, significant transformation have exhibited the following characteristics:

- Growth has been slower than they'd like, so some of the attorneys have ventured out to a few events to see if they can identify a few new clients on their own.

- A few clients have made comments about law firm websites being "from the '90s," so the firms are considering redesigns over the next several months.

- Attorneys have started to feel a bit self-conscious when they're bringing younger clients in for meetings; attorneys wonder what their practice looks like from this younger generation's perspective and how they might be able to improve this perception.

- They've heard internal grumblings about their technology for some time now, so they're starting to consider a switch to a more modern platform that might gain them some efficiencies.

- They get anxious about how long it takes to fulfill certain client requests and have started investigating where the bottleneck is in the process.

- They have tried-and-true methods, but realize that times change and they might need to as well.

- They've started asking other firms if they're experiencing similar challenges, and they are open to discussing potential solutions.

The more closely you can identify with that profile, the easier it's going to be for you to get your entire firm on board with our vision.

It's not within the scope of this book (or frankly of my expertise) for me to tell you how to build the "right" culture within your firm. It *is* within the scope for me to tell you that your culture can make or break this whole journey for you. If your firm is categorically opposed to change, you will not change.

Usually, the situation is not so extreme; although your firm probably doesn't rush willy-nilly toward the latest and greatest, a well-founded case to mix things up will at least be heard. Your first step is, naturally, to state your case to firm stakeholders. I hope to have provided enough big-picture evidence so that you can easily articulate what inaction could cost your firm (in concrete dollar amounts wherever possible) and what is to be gained by a firm-wide commitment to Exceptional Customer Service.

The *2018 Law Firms in Transition Survey* delivers this plea:[37]

> The recession was a 'known' event (albeit severe) to be endured and managed—as law firms had done in prior economic downturns. The threat in 2018 is broader and more nuanced, arising primarily from the sweeping force of technology evolution over the last two decades that has resulted in the commoditization and commercialization of more and more legal services.
>
> [...]
>
> Without a crisis, it's hard to create a sense of urgency. But waiting for a crisis is never a good strategy, as then any actions you take will come too late. Law firm leaders need to engage their influential partners now in the thoughtful consideration of current market change and likely future outcomes. Those partners need to care about the future of the firm—or, at the very least, get out of the way.

While I might not encourage anyone to "get out of the way," since I truly believe that any transition needs to be embraced (or at a minimum, tolerated) firm-wide in order to succeed, I completely agree with the overall sentiment here: now is the time to make waves, not later.

From there, more tactically speaking, one hugely effective method to kick-start your momentum is to *start with an easy win*. For a lot of firms, an easy win is going to take the form of stepping up your mobility game. The lack of mobility is a major source of friction both internally and externally; your team doesn't want to be tied to your physical office, and your clients won't likely put up with this sort of limitation either. (And I would venture to guess that your firm would be tickled to offer its attorneys the freedom to work and bill from anywhere.) In the next section, I'll get into the technical specifics of how to do this; the point here is to get your team's buy-in for technological change by showing them its efficacy in a way that benefits them personally. Eliminate barriers to mobility and flexibility, and the net result will be a team that is liberated, empowered, and eager to see the next development in your technology systems.

Who knows—they might become so enamored with this more modern, service-oriented way of working that they'll be the ones pushing *you* to move forward.

Solutions and Strategies

Y ou've gotten your house in order with regard to your T-OML, and you've primed the pump internally for the impending changes in how your attorneys and staff are going to work on a day-to-day basis. Now it's time to dive into the solutions and strategies you need to consider in order to bolster each of the pillars and to provide Exceptional Customer Service. My recommendations boil down to this:

Pillar	Solution/Strategy
Responsiveness	■ Beef up and prioritize your mobile strategy. ■ Employ collaboration tools for internal and external use.
Expertise	■ Use these collaboration tools. ■ Embrace video conferencing. ■ Tighten up your knowledge management strategy.
Results	■ Create a repeatable process to identify, track, and report meaningful results.
Innovation	■ Create a repeatable process to stay tuned into technology trends.

I'll dig into each of these in as much depth as I believe will be useful to you and to your firm's IT staff and partners.

Mobile Strategy

If your firm is to be responsive, its mobile strategy can no longer be an afterthought; instead, it must stand at the very core of your information systems. An effective mobile strategy takes the following into consideration:

1 Providing your attorneys and staff with the same work experience regardless of their location

2 Putting the right devices in play to set your mobile workforce up for success

3 Having the right infrastructure to support this style of work

Ask yourself: when you work from your desk and when you work from home, are the experiences the same?

It's not unusual for firms today to have one (productive) work experience in their offices and a completely different, secondary (less productive) experience anywhere else. Some firms will have their attorneys use LogMeIn or GoToMyPC to connect with their desktop computers. Those methods will be mostly functional, but in a fairly clunky and not entirely user-friendly way. Other firms will use Citrix or Terminal Services, and attorneys will have two entirely different "desktops." This kind of setup is preferable to one in which your attorneys can work *only* when they're physically in your office, but it won't be enough.

You can offer your attorneys and staff a seamless remote and mobile experience in a few ways, although all solutions will rely heavily on cloud computing. One approach is to combine a cloud-based email-and-productivity package like Microsoft Office 365 and cloud-based software applications for document management, case management, time and billing, and so forth. Another is to "rent" your servers from a cloud provider who will be the one responsible for maintaining and upgrading that hardware in their datacenter. A third is to go all in with a virtual-desktop solution, which means that your entire infrastructure—applications, servers, desktops, and all—lives with your provider.

To go about choosing the solution that will be the best fit for your firm, don't worry so much about comparing features or trying to parse through technical capabilities. What matters most are the business results that each solution can deliver to your firm. Some results to consider are:

- Freedom to work from anywhere, any time, on any device

- Freedom from investing in and maintaining hardware

- Minimal risk and responsibility

- Confidence that your privileged data is secure

- Trusted, reliable, round-the-clock technical support for your attorneys and staff

- An environment tailored to your firm's culture and workflow

- Financial predictability

Determine which of those are most important to your firm and which will bring you closest to delivering the level of responsiveness your clients won't be able to stop yammering about. Work with your IT team to match the appropriate solution(s) to those results.

Then, go one step deeper and think through which mobile devices you can and should support to run your key applications. If you want your attorneys to be able to serve your clients fully no matter where they happen to be located, assess their ability to accomplish core functions from outside the office. For example:

- Viewing and editing PDF files

- Securely accessing and sharing firm documents

- Collaborating on documents with other members of the firm

- Collaborating on documents with clients

- Filing documents

- Tracking time

- Accessing your docketing system

- Accessing client contact information

I'm sure you can think of additional functions. How well can you perform these tasks today? Which of these functions are imperative if you're looking to be truly responsive? Of those, which are the highest priority?

It will, of course, be your choice whether you want to (a) accommodate existing mobile devices and find solutions that are compatible with whatever devices your attorneys and staff happen to use, or (b) limit approved devices to a highly specific subset to simplify the required integrations and support burden. I tend to recommend the latter, as one of the most fundamental IT best practices is to streamline and simplify your technology environment as much as possible. It also makes security easier and helps unify everyone's work experience. But your decision will need to mesh with your culture.

Once you've established the capabilities you're looking to achieve and the devices you're willing to support, again work with your IT team to match the appropriate solutions, add-ons, and integrations to make it work.

You'll also need to make sure you have sufficient (and reliable) internet bandwidth in the places your team members work. As your firm moves more and more functions to the cloud in order to achieve the mobility and flexibility you're looking for, you're putting an increasingly heavy burden on your internet connections. If you don't take your bandwidth into account, you'll find yourself fighting against painfully slow performance that will hinder your team's productivity and negate all the benefits inherent in cloud computing.

Finally, make sure you create and enforce formal written policies and procedures detailing how your attorneys and staff are to work within this new flexible environment. These policies should include:

- **Telework policy.** How, where, and when are your attorneys permitted to telework? Your paralegals? Staff? Non-exempt employees?

- **Equipment use policy.** If your firm provides mobile devices, can these devices be used for personal matters? If your team uses personal devices, are they allowed to save firm documents on them? What are the parameters?

- **Bandwidth policy.** What's the minimum bandwidth your remote workers need to have to work effectively? Will your firm reimburse expenses?

Nail these policies down and wrap them into your technology strategy, your business strategy, and your new-employee onboarding routine.

Collaboration Tools

The practice of sending emails to multiple people and ending up with splintered and incoherent email chains is *not* collaboration. There's no timeliness there, and it's hard to keep your train of thought moving in an effective manner. When I talk about collaboration, I mean two things:

- You have an effective commenting and review cycle, and you can work through a document live with one or more people making changes during the discussion.

- You can easily discuss a case, client, or document and share both ideas and work product among members of your firm.

The idea is to eliminate as many barriers as we possibly can between your doing your work and your delivering that final work product to your client. This is exactly what lawyers sought to do with BlackBerrys years ago; they quickly realized that having mobile access to email would be a game changer as far as productivity and customer service were concerned. But while our smartphones now deliver our emails with nicer fonts and the ability to open attachments, it's really just an incremental improvement of the technology we've had for the past two decades. To make a real change in the way your firm is working, you have to look at communication through a different lens. We can do better than email now.

To reshape how your firm approaches communication, look into an all-in-one collaboration tool. Slack is the number-one contender in this space, and it's one of our core business applications at Optimal. This platform takes your internal conversations out of email and into a centralized, dynamic platform that combines instant messaging, voice calling, video calling, file sharing, and conversation threads that are reminiscent of social media.

Before we rolled out Slack, my inbox would consistently hover around three hundred emails, most of which were (splintered, inefficient) internal email chains about a client, a prospect, or a project. Today, it's rare for my messages to surge above forty. The other couple hundred messages are now organized and streamlined inside the appropriate threads within the appropriate channels in Slack. I can follow every new message in each thread and interact in real time, I can leave conversations to read at my leisure, and I can leave an entire channel at will. Our ability to quickly put our heads together and solve problems for our clients has gone through the roof. So too has our ability to disconnect from conversations that we don't need to be part of, that only divert our attention from more relevant matters.

In a law firm, a tool like this can do wonders for your efficiency. Say that two partners, two associates, and one paralegal are working together on a particular document for a client. How do they pass that document back and forth with changes? How do they comment on it? How do they debate specific legal points? Are most of the discussions taking place inside Word's commenting feature in a serial fashion as the document is passed from one person to another? Inside Slack, you can post a link to the document, have everyone jump into the document at the same time, and start a discussion in real time.

Say you need to get on the phone with all members of a particular client team. How convoluted is that process? Do you send an email and go back and forth and back and forth to find a time that works for everyone? Then schedule the call with a complicated dial-in number? What do you do when you're at home or traveling? Inside Slack, you could pop into that team's dedicated channel and (a) start a message thread to find a good time, (b) create a poll and solicit responses, or (c) click the phone icon to immediately start an audio or video call with everyone in that channel.

How much time could something like Slack save you? How many headaches?

Slack isn't the only player in this game, of course—another big player is Microsoft Teams, which is included with Microsoft's Office 365 suite. Microsoft marketed this product as a "Slack-killer," although I'm not so sure that will ever be the case. Personally, I don't believe that Teams is robust or user-friendly enough for the sort of work my company is doing, but this may not necessarily be the case for your firm, and I'm sure Microsoft will make improvements over time.

In fact, you may find that none of these packages are right for your firm and that you'd be better off using something else. Maybe your whole firm takes full advantage of collaboration functionality inside your document or case management system and doesn't need to introduce another package into the mix. Great! I'm not trying sell any of these products. I'm trying to sell the idea that there's a different, more effective way to work, and that it is worth your time to determine how you can introduce it into your firm. Since we can't manufacture time, we need to have the solutions and the processes in place that allow us to get more done over the course of a standard work day, without being distracted by the frenetic pace of dealing with overflowing email and voicemail inboxes. That's what these packages can do for you.

As an important note: When it comes to collaboration tools in particular, implementation *must* be handled very carefully in *all* situations. I've seen lots of failures when law firms and other companies try to implement these tools with no structure or planning. More to come on this later (see the "Implementation and Adoption" section).

Video Conferencing Platform

As we shift away from the silver service sets and mahogany bookcases, and as we embrace increasing amounts of remote and mobile work, we shift toward video conferencing software.

This concept itself is nothing particularly new; just as lawyers were early adopters of BlackBerrys, they realized a long time ago that they'd benefit from video conferencing technology. Big firms would drop $60,000 per office on Cisco TelePresence and set up all this equipment and a huge screen in their fancy conference rooms at all of their various locations. Then, when they needed to hold a meeting between their D.C. and California teams, each would congregate in their respective conference rooms, ~~offer a blood sacrifice to the capricious gods of telepresence,~~ fire up the technology, and carry on as if both groups were in one office.

Then Polycom got into the game and could offer this technology for half that price—which, of course, was still infeasible for most smaller firms. As recently as five years ago, we saw firms throwing tons of money at these high-tech video conferencing solutions for their offices. These aren't bad solutions, but since they're tied to your physical office, the uses are limited. Are you going to go into your conference room and have a formal teleconference with a lawyer who's traveling? Not likely—you'll opt for a phone call instead, and you'll lose the personal element that video provides.

And what are the chances that any of your clients will have access to this technology? Again, not likely—either you'll be relegated to a phone call, or one of you will need to travel to the other's place for an in-person meeting. In-person meetings, of course, are fantastic for client relations and satisfaction—but they don't always make for the most efficient use of time. Then, for more cost-sensitive clients, there is always the issue of who pays for travel. And phone calls to go over documents are particularly tedious when you have to guide your client through to the specific paragraph you are working on. There are significant efficiencies available in the market today, and you can put them to work sooner than your competitors for a win-win situation with your clients.

What we're looking for is a solution that will allow you to connect with your team and your clients as easily and as conveniently as we can connect with our friends and family using consumer packages like FaceTime, Skype, and WhatsApp. If I can video-chat with my daughter over Skype while she's at school in England, why can't I video-chat with a colleague who's working from home?

Over the past few years, the market has answered this call in the form of cloud-based video conferencing software that works on every device imaginable—and actually delivers significantly *better* quality than what we're seeing on the consumer side of things. A few platforms I'd recommend investigating are Zoom, BlueJeans, and Skype for Business (formerly Microsoft Lync and now part of Teams).

The first package, Zoom, is the solution we use internally and externally at Optimal. This is the most painless and seamless video conferencing platform I've encountered. Besides having exceptional voice and video quality, Zoom provides virtual conference rooms and screen-sharing to simulate most types of in-person interactions. Being able to work through a document with your client, with both of you literally on the same page, reading the same sections at the same time and having a real-time discussion about the content—no matter where either of you happens to be located—removes the clunky, frustrating back-and-forth from the picture altogether.

These solutions don't need to be expensive, and they don't need to be complicated. Zoom is a subscription service that, right now, is costing me less than $300 per month for my forty people; most of us are on the free Basic plan, while a few power-users on the Sales and Client Service side are on higher (paid) tiers. The only hardware investments you'll need to consider are for webcams and microphones if your machines aren't already equipped with those features (most laptops are, and most of these platforms have mobile apps that will tap into your phone or tablet without any hassle).

Do also keep in mind that this is a market that is in seemingly non-stop flux; solutions will regularly leapfrog each other, but none will fall too far behind the pack before catching back up. In other words, you'll probably be well served by any of these packages, as they don't vary dramatically. And, frankly, even a less-than-perfect video conferencing experience blows both traditional phone conferences and unnecessary face-to-face meetings out of the water.

One final note: Do not be discouraged if your clients don't take to video conferencing straightaway. My team has noticed an interesting phenomenon with adoption—the first few times you initiate a video call, your clients probably won't turn their cameras on. That's fine. Over time, if your attorneys keep using their cameras, clients will grow comfortable enough to turn theirs on, too—although perhaps with the camera pointing ever so slightly downward or to the side. As you continue to show your face, and as your client is able to establish a rapport with you, there will almost always come a day when you'll finally have a face-to-face virtual meeting. And the relationship you build with that client will be stronger than what you could establish as a disembodied voice over the phone.

Knowledge Management Strategy

One of the most effective ways to bolster your firm's expertise is to have a solid knowledge management strategy in place. This means that your people have the ability to catalog their work product and have that information readily available to others in the firm.

This is going to look different for different areas of law, but for many firms, your knowledge management strategy will be realized by way of a DMS. And for many firms, document management seems to be one area that has hardly changed at all over the years. There are both human and technical aspects to consider here.

For one thing, a full third of law firms are still using manual document management.[38] *A third!* How long must it take to locate one particular version of one particular file from one particular case from many years ago? How many times is this lengthy process repeated and by how many people over the course of a day, a week, a year? How easy is it to misplace a file? For files to become damaged by fire, flood, or otherwise? How secure are these documents? How much does it cost to store all these boxes of all these paper files? The risks to your productivity, your data, and your security are enormous.

For those firms that *are* using software packages to store and organize their files, they aren't always doing so very effectively. An International Data Corporation (IDC) study found that on average, information workers, including attorneys, lose 2.3 hours a week searching for *and never finding* digital files. Attorneys lose another 2 hours each week to re-creating files because they can't locate what they were looking for.[39] So we're talking about losing 4.3 hours per person, per week. What would that equate to in lost revenue for your firm?

All these documents being lost or misfiled could be the result of run-of-the-mill user error, of attorneys working around the system for any number of reasons, of the software itself not being intuitive enough, or a combination of all of the above. Regardless, the impact is the same: firms are losing their work product, and it's costing them money. Here's my recommendation:

- **If you don't have a DMS in place**, it's time to get one.

- **If you do have one**, make sure it's up-to-date and supported. More importantly, make sure it's working well for your people. Have you checked to see what add-ons and applications it might have that would be of use? Have people been trained on how to use it effectively? Consider surveying your staff to see what they might be frustrated with or confused about.

- **If your current solution is outdated or ineffective**, either fix it or get a new one.

If you find that you need to select and implement a software package like this, you must tread carefully; in the same way the right solution will amplify your productivity and effectiveness, an inadequate or poorly designed solution can cripple your firm's operations. When you're evaluating document management solutions, consider the following:

- **Structure.** Will the software take over your existing file structure? Will your documents be organized by matter? By client? By case? All three interchangeably?

- **Permissions.** To what extent can you customize user access? By matter? By client? By document?

- **Versioning.** Can you keep track of different versions of your documents? For how long? How are they stored and accessed?

- **Search capability.** Can you perform full-text searches? Are your searches based on tags? Fields? Both? How user-friendly is the search function?

- **File sharing.** Can you securely share documents with external users? Will your files be encrypted both in transit and at rest? Can you rescind a share? Track it?

- **Collaboration.** Can you discuss a particular document within the DMS itself? How intuitive is the setup? Can you generate document links to use inside your internal communication platform?

- **Compliance.** If you're subject to specific regulations (HIPAA, SEC, etc.), can your vendor guarantee compliance on their end? How do you know?

- **Billing integration.** Will the DMS integrate with your existing time-and-billing software (specifically, in updating your client and matter information)? Or will you need some custom programming?

- **Email integration.** Can you file emails directly in the package? How many steps does it take?

- **Mobile access.** Can you use the software from mobile devices? To what extent? Are there native apps for every operating system (Android, iOS)?

- **Reporting.** What are your reporting capabilities? How are these controlled? Who has access?

- **User interface.** What does the interface look like? Is it easy to navigate? Or will your attorneys need training to even get started?

- **Support.** If you run into trouble using the software, what are your options? Can you access a support team by phone or email? What are their hours? Are there limitations to what they'll do for you? Do you need to identify and rely upon local implementation and support partners?

- **Training.** What kind of training does the vendor offer to you and your firm? Any ongoing group training? Will it cost you extra?

- **Conversion planning and support.** How—precisely—will you move from your current situation into your new solution? Will you need to hire a third party to take you from design to follow-up? How long will the implementation process take, including a pilot phase for testing and customization?

- **Cost and pricing structure.** What exactly are your up-front and ongoing fees going to look like? Will you pay annually? Monthly? How often will you need to upgrade your licensing? Is this included in your ongoing fees?

When we walk our clients through this process, we'll typically create a matrix with the factors that are most important to them, write out what their ideal solution would look like (what capability is a must-have, what would be nice to have, and what they could do without), and record how the different solutions stack up. We'll go through vendor interviews and demos and try to get a sense of what each solution would look like in practice, not just in theory. It's a complex process, but it's absolutely necessary—I've seen an absurd number of failed DMS implementations, and the repercussions are *expensive*.

All told, you need to have a thoughtfully implemented, *fully adopted* solution where every document is stored within the platform—with the right security—and is accessible over the web and on your phone whenever and wherever you need it. It's well organized and flexible for everyone in your firm. It's mandatory so you don't have half the firm working around it and saving files to their local hard drives. It's a system that people find to be helpful rather than a hindrance.

If the solution is done right, both your team and your clients will thank you for it. If we can make all the expertise in the firm digitally available to every attorney in the firm, then we have given them a way to make that expertise available, quickly, to their clients. We aren't striving for perfection, but we can make some really good strides with the right knowledge management software.

Results Tracking

Here we're looking for an easy and repeatable way to quantify the value that you're providing to your clients. I'll bring back the example I mentioned before: my lawyer has a *100 percent win rate* on all collections activity for my company over the course of decades of working together. That's incredible! But right now, that's anecdotal evidence that I identified on my own and that he has no way to show his prospective clients unless I personally happen to tell them (which I've had exactly zero opportunities to do). What we're looking to do here is to create a process for:

1 Identifying the results you want to measure and how you will measure them

2 Collecting those measurements in some kind of centralized repository

3 Reporting those measurements to your current clients to demonstrate what you *have* achieved on their behalf

4 Communicating those measurements to your prospective clients to demonstrate what you *can* achieve on their behalf

To get a handle on what results your firm should be tracking, ask yourself what business value you're delivering to your clients and how you can measure your success in that regard. This task doesn't require any sort of complex number-crunching software that will spit out equally complex reports. This is more of an analytics question than it is a database question, and it can be as simple as a quick survey of your clients.

At Optimal—thanks to the wise consultation of my good friend and sales guru Ian Altman[40]—we've built various tracking mechanisms into our standard procedures, beginning during our sales process ("What would success look like to you six months down the road? How could we know for sure that we knocked it out of the park?") and spanning the course of our partnerships. We've found that one of the most effective forms of measurement has been using a simple 1-to-10 rating scale.

Say, for instance, that a new client has told us that their firm has completely lost faith in their technology support. We'll ask them to send a one-question survey to their attorneys and staff: *On a scale of 1 to 10, please rate how helpful IT services have been in supporting you in your work.* The average response gives us our baseline for firm confidence in their IT services. Then, six months later, we'll send out the same survey to measure our progress. Twelve months later, we'll send another. Just recently we polled a client of ours and were able to show them a 30 percent increase in overall staff confidence in their IT services since we first began serving them.

This sort of survey is also built into our executive-level Quarterly Business Reviews, in which we ask our clients to rate our overall service on a scale of 1 to 10 and explain the reasoning behind their answers. (The real value on the service delivery side is in the qualitative part of their response—that's where you'll find all your opportunities to improve the rating even more going forward.) All it took to track the information was adding a few new form fields into our existing CRM.

For your firm, a survey like this might do the trick. All you'll need to do to begin tracking your ratings is determine who's going to ask the question and when. Or, if your clients and prospects would respond better to results that speak to dollars saved and dollars earned, see if you already have the means of compiling that data. If not, identify a simple and repeatable process to get it going forward.

Technology will help you on the tracking front. These results can probably be tracked in a spreadsheet for smaller firms, and perhaps as fields in your DMS for a larger firm. Again, keep it simple and make it an internal process that happens whenever you close a file.

Once you've quantified the value you're delivering, communicate it to your clients and plaster those results in aggregate on your site, on your social media pages, in your marketing literature, and anywhere else you can think of. These sorts of metrics don't take a lot of time or effort to collect, and the effects are staggering from the standpoint of both attraction and retention.

Ongoing Technology Education

In order to stay in tune with the trends that are going to affect your firm and your clients, you'll need to invest time; unfortunately, there isn't a technology solution you can pop into place that will keep you up-to-date with technology. It could be your time that's invested. It could be an associate's time. It could be a consultant's time. Or, if your firm is large enough, it could be an internal or outsourced CIO's time. But it has to take *someone's* time. This is, unfortunately, an area where "learning by doing" doesn't apply; you can't just organically come up to speed on artificial intelligence or machine learning. Someone has to dedicate time to identifying the trends at hand, evaluating the ways those trends could affect your firm and/or your clients, and mapping out appropriate action plans.

More than implementing any solution, then, this pillar requires implementing a process to ensure that you can consistently identify the trends that are coming down the pike and determine which ones are worth your firm's attention. You can achieve this in a number of ways:

- Forming an internal Tech Committee, whose responsibilities include identifying areas of technology that are potentially relevant to the firm and worth exploring

- Attending technology webinars, seminars, and conferences

- Subscribing to newsletters and e-zines

- Seeing if your local Bar Association has a technology section you can join

- Contracting with an IT firm offering CIO services

- Contracting with an IT firm that keeps you up-to-date with periodic briefings, or tasking your internal team with the same initiative

Figure out what kind of approach makes the most sense given your firm's size and resources, and put the internal processes in place to wrap it into your standard operations.

When you identify a trend that could have a material impact on your ability to serve your clients better, commit resources to further research. Consider running a pilot with likely beneficiaries of the new technology as proof of concept before implementing it firm-wide.

If you happen to identify a trend that you want to turn into a new practice area, determine what it will take to become a leading resource in that field, and put the time in to make it happen.

Rinse and repeat.

Implementation
and Adoption

U nfortunately, you can't just throw all those solutions and strategies at the wall and have them stick. If you try that method, you'll fail spectacularly for two reasons:

1 Your team won't know *how* they're supposed to use the new solutions.

2 Your team won't know *why* they're supposed to use the new solutions.

In theory, all of the changes we're making are for the betterment of your attorneys and staff as individuals, and of your firm as a whole. You'll be able to get your work done more seamlessly, serve your clients more thoughtfully, and grow your firm more effectively. But change is uncomfortable. These new technologies will disrupt the way folks have been working at your firm—possibly the way things have been for decades. Even the most open-minded, tech-savvy group needs you to provide them with the tools to wield these new solutions and strategies confidently and with purpose. If you don't, you'll wind up with a portion of your team using a solution well, another portion using it poorly, and another portion rejecting it altogether. And that's not progress.

To get your firm aligned in support of these changes, you need to ensure that each solution is properly *implemented* from a technical standpoint and fully *adopted* from a cultural standpoint.

Thoughtful Implementation

For a new technology solution to be implemented properly, you have to consider how the solution itself works, how it will play with the other elements of your technology environment, and how your people will be using it. Much of this process will not (and should not) be your responsibility. But you should know whether or not your IT team is checking the right boxes along the way. From a high level, a good implementation project will include:

1 Research and planning (including compatibility and so forth)

2 Solution design (customizing the off-the-shelf product however necessary)

3 Testing, testing, testing

4 Communication with your firm (in plain English) about the changes ahead and how individuals will be affected

5 Training in advance of the "go-live" date

6 The scheduled "go-live"

7 Follow-up support and more training

The training piece of the puzzle will require your involvement. You'll need to set your folks up with training that (a) is commensurate with their abilities and (b) takes into account how different the new solution will look and feel compared to your current setup. If there's a sizeable learning curve, you'll need to invest more time in helping your people navigate the new territory. One of the best ways to do this is to involve a cross-section of your firm in various elements of the implementation project. In an article he published for the International Legal Technology Association,

"DMS Upgrade and Migration Lessons Learned," Frank Schipani digs into the twofold benefits of extensive up-front user involvement: a more tailored and user-friendly solution, and a dramatic head start toward firm-wide buy-in (i.e., better adoption).[41]

> There are few projects where user buy-in is more important than a DMS migration. "Make sure you take the time to do a pilot!" says Jim Struve of Belin McCormick, P.C. "Up-front involvement in configuration and buy-in from pilot partici-pants will help smooth the inevitable 'why can't I do [blank] like I used to?' complaints."
>
> It can be difficult to budget the time and effort required for pre-migration testing by users, but the payoff is well worth it. The folks who will use your DMS to its fullest, like paralegals, secretaries and associates, will find things in their testing that the technologists will never see. Their input is invaluable both for finding problems and for identifying areas where extra training or configuration may be needed to make the system more user friendly for the rest of the firm. As a bonus, any group that you involve in the initial design and testing phases can become champions of your project around the firm. Once people have had a hand in designing and planning, they then have a vested interest in seeing the project succeed. This will pave the way toward a successful migration and help take the edge off the inevitable bumps and problems you will encounter along the way.
>
> [...]
>
> And remember to promote and train on any features that are new to your firm. We held advanced training classes on NetDocuments' faceted search functions that helped people find the most difficult to find documents. People considered

these kinds of new features as a good tradeoff for having to learn a new system.

If you have an internal IT department, they should be able to orchestrate and execute this sort of pilot project for you. If you outsource, have your IT team give you a sense of how they'll run the project from both a technical and a communication standpoint, and make sure they're involving the right players at the right time.

From there, be sure that you have a resource at the ready to support you for the days, months, and years ahead. If your lawyers run into enough glitches, issues, or obstacles with a platform and they aren't quickly or effectively resolved, those lawyers are going to find a way to work around that platform. Then all the time and money you've invested in implementing this solution will be for naught.

Firm-Wide Adoption

When we switched to Slack for our internal communication at Optimal, we were changing the way the company had operated for over twenty years. We were *deeply* entrenched in email—all of our internal processes and procedures revolved around email as our primary form of communication, and although we all felt overwhelmed by the sheer quantity of messages that we received on a daily basis, we had adapted our way of work to fit that model. Had we installed Slack on everyone's machines and said "Have at it," guess how many of us would have defaulted right back to email? Enough to render the solution worthless.

In fact, that is exactly what happened to us a year prior. Our team had expanded to include more remote workers than we had ever had previously, and we had hoped to find a way to wrap those people into our company and our culture. One of our network engineers brought up Yammer, a Microsoft product reminiscent of a social media platform that could foster more centralized collaboration and team-building. We installed the platform, gave everyone in the company access, and told them to have fun. Another one of our engineers suggested that we use Microsoft Lync (now Skype for Business) for internal video calls as an alternative to the more impersonal options of instant messaging and phone calls. So we set everyone up with Lync accounts, too, and let the team know that this fun new capability existed.

And nothing changed.

Although the people in our company are savvy enough to figure out, within seconds, how all of these platforms work technically, *no one knew when to use what.* We now had information flowing in five separate places, with no clear parameters as far as what conversations were to take place where, or even what purpose each tool served. Within a few weeks, our team—overwhelmed and without guidance—abandoned the new technologies altogether and we were right back where we started.

So beyond the more tactical ability to use the tools your firm has put into place, it's *critical* to take the technology you're implementing and fold it into your operations and your firm culture. In a way, your goal is to interrupt the inertia that you've built over the years and to pointedly redirect your team to the new and improved ways of accomplishing their daily tasks.

In addition to potentially disrupting how your team has worked in the past, new solutions will also inevitably conflict with the way various members of your team would *prefer* to work. When you institute a change for your law firm, you're cutting across all sorts of technological sensitivities and familiarities. Some people (especially the younger crowd) will beg to do all of their work inside Google Docs. Some would happily live inside email for the duration of their tenure. Some will be die-hard Mac fanatics. Some will refuse to let go of their PCs. Some have spent their entire lives immersed in social media and are fluent in Snapchat and TikTok. Some were dragged onto Facebook by a family member but have never once logged in. What this means is that no matter what end of what spectrum your chosen solution falls on, a subset of your firm is going to feel uncomfortable with the change. This makes it even more difficult to unite your team collectively around *one* new platform, and this is precisely why it's so important to approach adoption with just as much care as you do implementation.

Unlike implementation, which is largely the responsibility of your IT team, successful adoption requires thoughtful and committed involvement from your firm; while you can work in concert with your IT team, they cannot accomplish this piece alone. When it comes to securing firm-wide adoption, here are some important steps for you to take:

1 **Get your firm leadership 100 percent on board.** This is the most critical aspect of successful adoption. Firm leadership should understand the problem you're working to solve, buy in all the way, and be the primary advocates of the new platform. If you include a cross-section of your firm in the implementation process, the partners must be involved.

2 **Communicate your intentions clearly.** Why is the firm implementing this solution? How, specifically, will this solution better allow you to deliver Exceptional Customer Service to your clients? How will you measure its effectiveness over time? Make sure your team understands *why* this change is taking place to begin with, and address any of their thoughts or concerns early on.

3 **Mirror your culture.** Wherever possible, design your solutions to fit your firm, not the other way around. If your firm has a culture of transparency, collaboration, and fun, your solutions should facilitate that style of work. If your firm is more regimented, your technology should reinforce those boundaries. A mismatch here will only confuse your team and hamper firm-wide adoption of the solution.

4 **Formalize (and enforce) Rules of the Road.** After you've established how you're going to use this solution internally in a way

that fits your culture, any rules, guidelines, and recommendations concerning the usage of the new solution need to be codified in a formal document and distributed to everyone in your firm. Then any deviation should be corrected without exception. The moment you let one finicky partner set their own standard, the whole construct will fall apart.

5 **Burn your bridges.** The day we officially launched Slack (after completing all of our internal training), we uninstalled our legacy instant messaging platform, Lync, and Yammer, thereby shifting all of those functions into Slack. Old habits die hard, so remove as much temptation to revert as you can.

6 **Train from Day 1.** Any new associates, attorneys, or staff that you bring aboard need to get the full picture: what solutions you're using, why you're using them, how the firm uses them, and what your expectations will be. Share any policy or "Rules of the Road" documents with them. Share recordings of your internal training sessions. Get them entirely up to speed from the get-go.

7 **Measure success.** Keep formal tabs on whether or not the solution is delivering your intended results. This monitoring will give you insight into how well the solution is performing, give you the opportunity to make adjustments as needed, and reinforce the "why" throughout your firm.

Beyond these steps, seize all opportunities you have to reinforce how and why to use the solution, and to solicit feedback from your team on where you might be able to make tweaks and improvements. We've done this in the form of infographics, lunch-and-learns, Q&A sessions, surveys, and more. Stay creative and stay consistent.

With thoughtful approaches to both the technical and human implications of the changes in store for your firm, you'll be in the perfect position to empower your team to provide Exceptional Customer Service, to delight your clients with every interaction, and to navigate this shifting landscape we're in with total mastery. The contrast between the work your firm is doing and the work your competitors are doing will be nothing short of remarkable.

The Last Word

In the summer of 2015, we rounded up the entire Optimal team at the Washington Sailing Marina in Alexandria for our biannual company Spirit Day. We broke off into groups of five or six and sailed the Potomac, an activity as challenging as it was fun—the near total absence of wind notwithstanding. After we wrapped up the team-building with a hilariously uneventful "race" (I don't think any of us actually managed to cross the finish line without paddling), we docked our boats and grabbed our commemorative Summer Sailing Camp T-shirts. The message printed on the back was this:

You can't change the wind, but you can adjust your sails.

If you feel a bit out of breath at this point, you're right to; based on what I've proposed, the road ahead is long and fraught with complex technological, operational, and cultural change. And in striving to provide you with the tools to address every part of this multi-year transition from start to finish, I leave you with more than most can comfortably swallow. Some readers threw this book down long ago, knowing full well this charge is too bold for their firm to take on. But if you've made it this far, and if you see value in this vision we've built together, the progress you've already made toward a thriving future is significant.

We can't control the landscapes in which we do business. We can't halt the exponential rate of technology innovation, and we can't will society to calm its collective demand for instant gratification.

But we can control how we respond.

It's my hope that rather than continuing business as usual, hoping that your firm can hunker down and weather this mounting storm, you will make the hard choice to actively and deliberately harness this new normal to your competitive advantage.

I hope you'll adjust your sails.

Acknowledgments

There are *so* many people I'd love to name. I'll do my best to acknowledge everyone here and will unabashedly grovel at the feet of anyone I realize post-publishing that I have ever so rudely forgotten.

To Frank Schipani, Seth Berenzweig, Roy Niedermayer, Michael Gottlieb, Nikki Korson, and Those Who Must Not Be Named: Thank you for allowing me to pick your brilliant brains for this book—I could not have pulled this together without your insight!

To Catherine Oliver: Thank you for one of the most enjoyable introductory calls ever, for helping me understand what "writing a book" actually means, and for your outstanding editing work that made me look like I know what I'm doing with all this.

To Ian Altman: Thank you for the wild idea to pull this book together and for convincing me to get it done—something my collection of "works in progress" proves is no easy feat.

To my colleagues and friends at Optimal: Thank you for your support, your wisdom, your honesty, your patience, your humor, your commitment, and your understanding. I could not be more proud to work alongside each of you.

To David Campbell: Thank you for helping me realize what an amazing effort this would be and for throwing gas on the fire whenever the flames started to wane.

To Lauren Meinecke: Thank you for the hours and hours and days upon days of help with research, writing, editing, gentle (and strong) encouragement, and just about anything one could ever imagine that goes into such an endeavor.

To the Association of Legal Administrators Capital Chapter: Thank you for providing me with such a warm and welcoming community to learn from and—if I'm doing this thing right!—contribute to. I can't wait for our next event together!

To the LinkedIn community: Thank you for all the comments and messages where you offered your feedback on my ideas and contributed some supremely valuable nuggets of your own.

To my wife, Melissa (who already has two spectacular and inspiring books under her belt), to Shari and Adam, and to my parents: Thank you for the encouragement, guidance, and support along the way.

Sources

1   Kent, Kevin. "83 Percent of Clients Now Look at Lawyer Reviews." *ReviewTrackers*, 3 Aug. 2015, www.reviewtrackers.com /lawyer-legal-professional-eye-lawyer-review-sites/.

2   Berenzweig, Seth. Partner, Berenzweig Leonard, LLP. Interview with the author.

3   Niedermayer, Roy. Principal, Paley Rothman. Interview with the author. March 16, 2018.

4   McSpadden, Kevin. "Science: You Now Have a Shorter Attention Span Than a Goldfish." *Time,* 14 May 2015, time.com/3858309 /attention-spans-goldfish/.

5   Reports and Data. "Chatbot Market Analysis, By Platform (Web Based, Mobile Based), By Type (Software and Services), By Industry Verticals (Creams & Ointments, Oral), By End User, By Application and By Region, Forecasts to 2026." Aug. 2019, www.reportsanddata.com/report-detail/chatbot-market.

6   "Immediate Need for Flawless Mobile Experiences – Think with Google." www.thinkwithgoogle.com/consumer-insights /consumer-immediate-need-mobile-experiences/.

7   Streitfeld, David. "Amazon Hits $1,000,000,000,000 in Value, Following Apple." *The New York Times*, 4 Sept. 2018, www.nytimes.com/2018/09/04/technology/amazon-stock-price -1-trillion-value.html.

8   Friedman, Thomas L. *Thank You for Being Late: An Optimist's Guide to Thriving in the Age of Accelerations*. Thorndike Press, a Part of Gale, Cengage Learning, 2017.

9   "Venture Capital Firms Go Deep and Wide with Blockchain Investments." *Diar*, vol. 2, no. 36, 1 Oct. 2018, diar.co/volume-2-issue-39/.

10 Friedman, Thomas.

11 Altman Weil, Inc. "Law Firms in Transition 2018: An Altman Weil Flash Survey." www.altmanweil.com//dir_docs/resource /45F5B3DD-5889-4BA3-9D05-C8F86CDB8223_document.pdf.

12 Friedman, Thomas.

13 Altman Weil, Inc.

14 "Three Myths of the '67 Percent' Statistic." SiriusDecisions. www.siriusdecisions.com/blog /three-myths-of-the-67-percent-statistic.

15 "Measuring Your Mobile Website Speed – Think with Google." www.thinkwithgoogle.com/marketing-resources /data-measurement/mobile-site-speed-tools/.

16 Altman Weil, Inc.

17 Ernst & Young. "Global Generations: A Global Study on Work-Life Challenges Across Generations." 2015, www.ey.com/us/en/about-us/our-people-and-culture /ey-work-life-challenges-across-generations-global-study.

18 Sujansky, Joanne G., and Jan Ferri-Reed. *Keeping the Millennials: Why Companies Are Losing Billions in Turnover to This Generation, and What to Do about It*. Wiley, 2009.

19 Deal, Jennifer J., and Alec Robert Levenson. *What Millennials Want from Work: How to Maximize Engagement in Today's Workforce.* McGraw-Hill Education, 2016.

20 PwC. "Millennials at Work: Reshaping the Workplace." www.pwc.de/de/prozessoptimierung/assets/millennials-at-work-2011.pdf.

21 Levin, Mark, and Bruce MacEwen. "Assessing Lawyer Traits & Finding a Fit for Success." http://therightprofile.com/wp-content/uploads/Attorney-Trait-Assessment-Study-Whitepaper-from-The-Right-Profile.pdf.

22 Gallup, Inc. "How Millennials Want to Work and Live." www.gallup.com/workplace/238073/millennials-work-live.aspx.

23 Gallup, Inc. "How to Tackle U.S. Employees' Stagnating Engagement." news.gallup.com/businessjournal/162953/tackle-employees-stagnating-engagement.aspx.

24 Rheem, Don. *Thrive by Design: The Neuroscience That Drives High-Performance Cultures.* ForbesBooks, 2017.

25 Altman Weil, Inc.

26 Legal Executive Institute. "2019 Report on the State of the Legal Market: Growing Competition Challenging Long-Held Law Firm Assumptions." www.legalexecutiveinstitute.com/2019-legal-market-report/.

27 Berenzweig, Seth.

28 Niedermayer, Roy.

29 Legal Executive Institute. "2017 Report on the State of the Legal Market." www.legalexecutiveinstitute.com/wp-content/uploads/2017/01/2017-Report-on-the-State-of-the-Legal-Market.pdf.

30 Legal Executive Institute. "2018 Report on the State of the Legal Market: Transformation of Legal Services Market Is Accelerating – Are Law Firms Ready?" www.legalexecutiveinstitute.com/2018-legal-market-report/.

31 Schipani, Frank. Director of IT and Operations, Three Crowns LLP. Interview with the author. March 13, 2018.

32 Gottlieb, Michael. Founder, Momentum Law Group. Interview with the author. March 13, 2018.

33 Berenzweig, Seth.

34 Altman Weil, Inc.

35 Gottlieb, Michael.

36 The Operational Maturity Level concept is copyrighted by Service Leadership Incorporated. The Technology Operational Maturity Level (T-OML) model is copyrighted by Optimal Networks, Inc.

37 Altman Weil, Inc.

38 "Study reveals lack of technological nous could waste weeks of fee-earner's time every year." 10 October 2013, legal.thomsonreuters.com.au/about-us/news /study-reveals-lack-of-technological-nous-could-waste-weeks.aspx.

39 IDC. "Bridging the Information Worker Productivity Gap in Western Europe: New Challenges and Opportunities for IT." 2012, denalilabs.com/static/ProductivityWhitepaper.pdf.

40 Altman, Ian, and Jack Quarles. *Same Side Selling: A Radical Approach to Break through Sales Barriers.* IdeaPress Publishing, 2014.

41 Schipani, Frank. "DMS Upgrade and Migration Lessons Learned." 15 May 2018, www.iltanet.org/blogs/frank-schipani/2018/05/17 /dms-upgrade-and-migration-lessons-learned?ssopc=1.

About the Author

Born in Israel, Heinan Landa made the trip to the States at the ripe old age of two. Here his parents built a successful instrumentation company, which they just recently sold after almost forty years in business.

After earning his B.S. and M.S. in Electrical Engineering and Computer Science from Johns Hopkins University, Heinan went on to receive his MBA from the Wharton School of Business at the University of Pennsylvania. As fate would have it, it was an assignment for one of his classes at Wharton that prompted him to develop the idea—and even construct a business plan—for his future technology services firm.

When Heinan graduated, he immediately set out to make his mock business plan a reality. He set up shop in one of his parents' vacant offices, hung up a self-constructed banner that read "Optimal Networks," and began calling organizations to gauge their interest in managed network support services.

While he was soon able to find a handful of clients and hire an employee, it was difficult not to feel defeated as a twenty-eight-year-old newlywed, living in an apartment with more than $100,000 in debt and drawing an annual salary of $35,000. But when he came home from work one night, more tempted than ever to throw in the towel, his wife was elated as she gave him the good news: he was going to be a father! (*AHH!*) After some serious thought, this defining moment prompted him to commit 100 percent to the success of Optimal Networks. His plan? Immerse himself in the area in which he was struggling—sales.

The next year, Optimal hit the $1 million mark.

Since 1991, Optimal has helped more than five hundred clients with their technology needs, all while maintaining an aggressive commitment to unyielding integrity, mind-blowing customer service, and some good old-fashioned fun.

When Heinan is not leading this merry band of self-professed Optimalites, you can find him at his home in Rockville with his wife Melissa and two kids, Shari and Adam.

…Actually, more likely, you'll find Adam studying at the University of Maryland or playing a gig with his band. Shari will likely be overseas attending lectures at Oxford or gallivanting around an opera house in London. Melissa will be at home writing her next book, or in a classroom teaching. Heinan could be in any of these places, or getting reenergized at the gym.

He's always up for a chat about business, technology, corporate culture, nutrition, both the Marvel and DC universes, and all things Mr. Spock, so feel free to drop him a note at hlanda@optimalnetworks.com or www.linkedin.com/in/hlanda/.

Additional Resources

To download printable copies of all graphics—including the T-OML Self-Assessment—and to access exclusive additional content, visit:

www.modernlawfirmbook.com

About Optimal Networks, Inc.

S ince 1991, the Optimal team has helped small to mid-sized law firms in the D.C. Metro area and beyond fuel their goals by way of thoughtful technology solutions and white-glove support. Three things make us different: our culture, our focus, and our services.

Culture Designed to Attract and Retain Top Talent

We've spent nearly three decades building and maintaining a culture of integrity, of service, and of fun. We take resolving important problems for our clients as seriously as we take cooking breakfast for our team every Friday morning in our office kitchen. We love technology, we love helping people, we love food, and we love dancing.

Our culture has been featured in *Inc. Magazine*, *Forbes*, *TechBisnow*, and *SmartCEO*, and we've won over a dozen awards at the local and national levels. The best testament, however, is probably the Scrapbook page on our website, which you can find at www.optimalnetworks.com /company/scrapbook/

The end result is a sky-high retention rate and a team that is engaged, happy, and all the more committed to taking the absolute best care of each and every one of our clients. In fact, at the time of writing, our team has a combined tenure of over 200 years!

Measurable Business Impact

We feel very strongly that the solutions and services we provide should have a measurable impact on our clients' businesses. Before beginning any new engagement, we take care to establish a shared definition of "success" with our clients and to map out how we will chart our progress toward this shared vision. If a successful partnership would result in increased staff confidence in your IT systems, for example, we may measure our progress by delivering a survey to staff at the beginning of our relationship, and then again six months in. Did their perception change? How? If not, how can we best redirect our efforts? When will we take our next measurement? This process keeps us focused on delivering the results that are important to you (not what we assume you might want) and allows us both to hold our team accountable.

Comprehensive Service Mix

Our services run the gamut from traditional managed services to on-site support to a preeminent corporate cloud solution to CIO consulting services. This means that rather than trying to force-fit our clients into one support model, we have the ability to provide them with whatever combination of services makes the most sense for them. As their needs evolve over time, so too can the ways we support and advance their technology (and, ultimately, their firms).

Problems We Solve for Law Firms

Naturally, we aren't the right provider for everyone. Our law firm clients tend to come to us when:

- Their partners or administrators are wasting time overseeing their IT operations when they could be advancing the firm's business goals instead.

- The firm is struggling to support remote and highly mobile workers, which frustrates both their employees and their clients.

- No one in the firm can confidently answer client questions about how the firm keeps sensitive data secure.

If a firm you know happens to be struggling with any of these challenges, we'd love to speak with them and see if we might be able to help.

www.optimalnetworks.com | 240-499-7900
info@optimalnetworks.com